A Quick Guide to Zotero 7

The Genohistory Quick Guide Series

A Quick Guide to

Zotero 7

Knowledge Management in Genealogy, History, and Other Fields

Donna Cox Baker

Golden Channel Publishing
Anniston, Alabama

Published in the United States of America by Golden Channel Publishing, Anniston, Alabama. Cover designed by author using ChatGPT 4o elements.

Zotero is an ongoing Corporation for Digital Scholarship project, which emerged from the Roy Rosenzweig Center for History and New Media at George Mason University. Plugins mentioned are usually developed by independent volunteers. This book is independently produced and is not a publication by any of these institutions.

Zotero is a trademark of the Corporation for Digital Scholarship. Golden Channel Publishing is trademarked by its owner, Donna Cox Baker. Baker coined the term "genohistory" but does not intend it to be trademarked by herself or anyone else, so long as it is presented as the study of an interconnected group of people, often a family or community, within the context of its own time and place.

ISBN 978-0-9996899-4-3
LCCN 2024930318.

GCP: 2024082301.02P

Golden Channel Publishing
234 Drennen Drive
Anniston, Alabama 36205-4418

Table of Contents

EXERCISES

PREFACE AND ACKNOWLEDGEMENTS

While I wrote this primer to serve my colleagues in the genealogy, history, and genohistory fields, it can be equally valuable to researchers from virtually all disciplines. Welcome, all. I am convinced Zotero is a researcher's essential companion.

To be concise—essential in a QUICK GUIDE—I limit my acknowledgments to Zotero's core team. Thank you to its developers and all who run the Corporation for Digital Scholarship. Their work contributes to global knowledge expansion. For individual acknowledgments, see Zotero's CREDITS AND ACKNOWLEDGMENTS[1] page.

---

1. INTRODUCTION TO ZOTERO 7

I discovered Zotero in graduate school when I desperately needed a tool for research and writing in history. I needed a place to store, organize, retrieve, and cite knowledge. I tried many options, including a homegrown Access database and expensive citation management tools that always disappointed me. Then a colleague recommended Zotero. I was skeptical about a free tool, but Zotero surprised me. Seventeen years later, it continues to enhance my effectiveness, efficiency, and creative thinking as a researcher. It even keeps surprising me. Zotero 7 was the best surprise yet.

My goal with this book is to get you started quickly, avoiding the mistakes I made when I began using Zotero so long ago without a guide or teacher. I want to save you time by guiding you through Zotero's features. For experienced users, I trust this guide will also be valuable. I spent months following the Zotero forums in preparation for this third book on Zotero. And I kept learning new things.

This book can't cover everything about Zotero, which is constantly evolving. However, within a few hours, you'll know enough to improve your research skills.

THE WHAT AND WHY OF ZOTERO

Robust and straightforward, Zotero helps you gather, arrange, store, cite, annotate, and collaborate in handling research information. I consider it my KNOWLEDGE MANAGEMENT SYSTEM. I use it for almost everything I want to recall in professional research, business, and life.

Zotero offers structure and flexibility for managing knowledge, allowing you to turn ideas and information fragments into polished and cohesive output. It combines the structured approach of a citation database with the flexibility of freeform notetaking software like Evernote and OneNote.

As a CITATION MANAGEMENT tool, Zotero supports bibliographic style standards and offers over 10,000 style variations. It streamlines the citation process, saving time and effort. You can create and organize notes, attach or link to various materials, accessing them anywhere with internet service.

With Zotero, you can create voluminous plain or formatted notes that are fully searchable and organized to suit your filing and display preferences. You can attach or link to material in numerous forms—documents of various types, spreadsheets, images, videos, audio files, web pages, and more. You can pull in entire books and articles, mark them up, and access them wherever you have a computer with internet service.

As OPEN-SOURCE software, Zotero's code is accessible and can be supplemented with plugins.[1] This allows for continuous improvement and the addition of new features by developers worldwide.

CHANGES IN ZOTERO 7

As I put the finishing touches on this book, Zotero 7 has been formally released for only 13 hours. I have had full access to the beta version in progress and have learned much by listening to the forum chatter of the beta testers and developers. While I am doing my best to give you the latest information, by the time you get it, it might have features that are not there yet. Zotero's development team continually improves the product. Visit the ZOTERO VERSION HISTORY[2] page regularly to get up-to-date information.

For those familiar with Zotero 6, the most significant changes in Zotero 7 lie in the user interface design, architectural infrastructure, ZOTERO READER, and plugins, with many great miscellaneous surprises spread throughout. You may view Zotero's announcement of the Zotero 7 release at ZOTERO 7: ZOTERO, REDESIGNED.[3]

If you have the 32-bit version of Zotero 6 on your computer and use the automated update feature in Zotero's HELP menu to upgrade to Zotero 7, you will probably upgrade to a 32-bit Zotero 7. If you want to upgrade to the 64-bit version (recommended), go to WWW.ZOTERO.ORG, and download and install the new version. (See EXERCISE 1 for details.)

---

[1] Language purists prefer the hyphenated "plug-ins," but I have chosen to use the form that appears on Zotero's interface.

[2] https://www.zotero.org/support/changelog

[3] https://www.zotero.org/blog/zotero-7/

Major User Interface Overhaul

The most noticeable innovation with Zotero 7 will be the redesigned workspace that looks refreshingly modern and has many eagerly awaited features embedded. The changes, while significant, will not require major relearning for current users.

Item Details

- The Item Details tabs that once lined the top of the right-most pane have been recast as collapsible sections, with a set of icons down the right edge of the pane. This allows developers to expand functions in future releases, without crowding the interface.

- A new header field has been added to the top of the Item Details pane. Bold and eye-catching, you have choices about what you want to appear in it: a Title; the Title, Creator, and Year; or its Bibliography Entry. To select your preference, right-click in the field and choose View As. The sentence casing feature has been improved in this field to eliminate inaccurate capitalization.

- In the Creator field, Zotero 7 allows you to Fix Case when the capitalization of a creator's name is incorrect. You can either right-click on the field or use the "..." menu at the end of the field line.

- A Libraries and Collections section reveals locations where an item is stored in My Library.

- The Attachment Section includes a large thumbnail of images or covers of your PDFs, EPUBs, and HTML snapshots, allowing you to see if you have located the intended document.

Search Capabilities

Zotero 7 includes new search features.

- We can search open Zotero Reader tabs by Title and reorder or close them quickly from the search window.

- A new search field has been placed in the COLLECTIONS pane to allow searching for collections in the main workspace, using any term within a collection title.
- The ADVANCED SEARCH feature is now included in the main search menu above the ITEM LIST. It includes the new capability of picking columns, as in the ITEM LIST.
- The SETTINGS can now be full-text or keyword searched.

ACCESSIBILITY IMPROVEMENTS

- Zotero 7 allows dark screen viewing and can follow the choices you have made on your computer regarding screen darkness. It is also available for viewing PDFs and EPUBs.
- You may choose a COMPACT or a COMFORTABLE (looser) layout density to quickly change how much material appears on your monitor.
- Keyboard navigation has been improved to promote accessibility.
- Greater support has been added for screen readers.
- More changes are in the works and will be rolled out in the months ahead, as completed.

ARCHITECTURAL IMPROVEMENTS

- The system architecture has changed to modernize and maximize Zotero's performance, speed, OS compatibility, and PDF and large file handling.
- Zotero 7 offers native support for Apple Silicon Macs, 64-bit Windows, and Windows on ARM to provide a seamless operation on new hardware.
- These changes lay the groundwork for other future improvements in a rapidly changing technological environment.

ZOTERO READER

Zotero 6 included a new PDF READER—a welcomed improvement. Now called ZOTERO READER, it offers much more.

- Zotero 7 brings new forms of annotation for PDFs, including ink drawing (formerly only on iOS), underlining, and text boxes. Text boxes can now be resized, expanding all contents as they grow. Highlights and underlines can now span a two-page spread.

- Annotation tools (highlights, underlines, and text boxes) are available for EPUB documents and HTML snapshot files. You no longer must save web pages as an awkwardly formatted PDF to be capable of marking up text. (Use of the snapshot capability will need paid storage—but it is worth the investment for so many reasons.)

- ZOTERO READER will attempt to extract a table of contents for a document, based on the styles within it. The table of contents will display in the left sidebar of the ZOTERO READER, using the second view button on the second toolbar row.

- PDFs can be opened in a separate window or in the ZOTERO READER. You can set a default behavior in EDIT > SETTINGS > GENERAL > READER.

- Hovering your cursor over a link will bring up a popup containing the citation or figure.

- A document view may be split horizontally or vertically, with both sections being fully functional.

- EPUBs and HTML snapshots are now included as READER options.

- The ability to condense individual annotations into a single comprehensive note has been moved into the READER as a standard tool.

- EPUBs with metadata can generate a parent citation item, and Zotero plans soon to make it possible to download EPUBs through the ZOTERO CONNECTOR.

- Combined with a plugin called BETTER NOTES (which will be described in a future Quick Guide), the ZOTERO READER is a game changer for researchers.

- Tabs have been added to allow multiple documents to be opened simultaneously. The tabs can be rearranged and, in the case of many, searched for by clicking the small down arrow at the right end of the tab bar.

- Annotations and notes that are extracted using the READER tools are linked back to their place in a document. If you click on a citation for text extracted from an annotation, the system will jump to the annotation in the attachment.

THIRD-PARTY PLUGINS

The architecture used for third-party developers to integrate plugins that expand Zotero's capabilities has been remodeled. It will make development easier and more stable across Zotero updates. This has been a major change to existing architecture, and some Zotero 6 plugins will not be available in version 7, if the developer has not been able to make the revisions. Zotero has worked to integrate many of the most widely used functions that are discontinued with the new release. Some plugin developers intend to bring their software up to the new Zotero 7 standard but are not there yet.

Two of the most popular discontinued Zotero 6 plugins are ZOTFILE and ZUTILO. Zotero has replaced much of what ZOTFILE did with built-in features. A new plugin called ACTIONS AND TAGS FOR ZOTERO replaces much of what ZUTILO did and adds much value beyond that.

A new plugin called ADD-ON MARKET FOR ZOTERO creates a menu of known plugins and allows you to set up automatic updates. If you set up this plugin first, you will not need to download most other plugins from remote sites.[4] It will also let you know which plugins are ready for Zotero 7. You are encouraged to contact the owners of any of your preferred plugins that appear to be unready, asking if you will need to find alternatives.

MISCELLANEOUS SURPRISES

The Zotero team has added or modified many functions to give users what they have requested in the online forums. While I will not

---

[4] https://github.com/syt2/zotero-addons#readme

detail them here, you will find some throughout this book and others as you stumble upon them in your work. Here are some of the most significant:

WORD PROCESSING ADD-ON IMPROVEMENTS

The red bar that opens when you seek to retrieve a citation from Zotero into your word processor has been redesigned to be more intuitive. It knows what item you last accessed in Zotero. It brings that item to the top of your drop-down list of potential citations. It pulls other open documents to the list just behind the active one. This speeds up your choice of a citation source and reduces the likelihood that you will choose the wrong one among same-named sources.

SENDING COLLECTIONS AND SAVED SEARCHES TO THE TRASH

COLLECTIONS and SAVED SEARCHES will no longer be lost when you have inadvertently sent them to the TRASH. Like items, you will now have the chance to find them in the TRASH and restore them until you have emptied it.

TAG EMOJIS IN ITEM LIST WITHOUT COLOR CODING

The use of a tiny symbolic icon known as an "emoji" on a tag label now causes Zotero to put the emoji as a flag on this item in the ITEM LIST—no longer requiring you to use a color tag.

NOTES WITH DICTIONARY CAPABILITIES

You can now add words to the dictionary of your chosen language in Zotero's notetaking features. You right-click in a NOTE, choose LANGUAGES, and then ADD/CHANGE DICTIONARIES to select your language. If Zotero does not recognize a term, it will mark it with a wavy red line beneath the problematic term. Right-click on that, and you can either choose the correct term of add the term to the dictionary if it is what you intended.

File Renaming Improvements

Zotero 7 expands the existing capacity to rename attachment files as you bring them into Zotero. You can use simple coding to choose what information is drawn from the parent metadata, its order, and any text or symbols you wish to use to separate things. A PDF's title in Zotero will be "PDF" unless you have altered it previously.

Troubleshooting Mode

Zotero 7 has added a HELP menu option to aid in isolating problems in the software. The RESTART IN TROUBLESHOOTING MODE option temporarily disables all plugins so you can determine if a problem is due to Zotero or one of its plugins.

Timeline Feature Removed

The TIMELINE feature is discontinued with Zotero 7. It was developed for a very specific use many years ago and has been rarely used recently. I plan to publish a Quick Guide soon that will demonstrate how I create timelines using Zotero's available features.

ABOUT THIS BOOK

I have designed this book to be a quick read, in hopes that most readers will go through it thoroughly. Experienced users will find new tips and features, even if they don't need to do the exercises. For beginners, a free sample data set is provided for practical exercises. (See Exercise 3 for instructions.)

In my earlier books, I went through the frustrating and complex work of doing very different formats of the book for print and e-book readers. Now wiser for wear, I have done what I can to make this book easily convertible to either type of reader. For links to web pages, which print edition readers cannot click, I include a footnote containing the URL address behind any links.

FOR THE E-BOOK VERSIONS

This book was designed to function with all commonly used e-readers, but it will be at its best with the newer ones that can reproduce fonts in SMALL CAPS, which I use on labels of screen elements and other key terms throughout. (The term "small caps" should appear different than the rest of this paragraph in the previous sentence, if your device supports this format.) It will also appear best with a reader app that can display emojis, special symbols, and colors. I recommend either the newest Kindle app or Google's Play Books—both of which are great to read even on a smartphone and are free to download.

As you do the exercises in this book, it would be ideal to have both the book and your Zotero software visible simultaneously. You might view the exercises on a tablet or smartphone to free up your computer. Or, if you are on a full-size monitor or have dual monitors, you might open the book in a narrow window beside your open Zotero window.

If the images appear small on your device, there are a couple of things to try:

- On hand-held devices, turn the device to landscape view.

- On touch devices, tap, double-tap, or hold on the image, then stretch it with your fingers, if needed.

- If you are viewing the EPUB version, set your device to scroll rather than paginate your content.

EPUB readers will have the wonderful luxury of pulling the book into Zotero, which launches its EPUB reader with version 7. You can mark the book up, annotate it, and have it constantly at hand as you work in Zotero.

OTHER QUICK GUIDES

When I began this book, it was not going to be a QUICK GUIDE. But as I discovered more and more of Zotero's secrets, it began to expand. My outline was growing daily. I feared Release 7 would be obsolete before you ever saw the finished product. Midway through, I decided to break up the material.

This is the first and foundational guide, but there should be more following soon behind. Some will be very specific to genealogy, history, and genohistory. But several, at least, will have a universal application to most researchers. Some will be basic and some more advanced. If you wish to be notified of Zotero-related developments, including training options, sign up for my EMAIL LIST FOR ZOTERO USERS.[5]

SOFTWARE VARIATIONS

Zotero supports Windows (including ARM), macOS, Linux, and iOS operating systems, and it can be set up on x86_64 Chromebooks. An Android version is nearing completion, having launched beta testing early in 2024. To be concise, I will write about Zotero as most users see it, on Windows, except in cases of notable differences.

INSTALLATION

Zotero offers a straightforward installation, which will work much like other standard installations on your computer.

EXERCISE 1. DOWNLOAD AND INSTALL ZOTERO

A CAUTION ABOUT CLOUD STORAGE: Do not install Zotero's programs or stored data in a cloud location. This can lead to data corruption if changes are made before syncing is complete. Install Zotero to its default location on your device's hard drive and perform regular backups using whatever tool you use for the rest of your computer software. In Chapter 4, I'll discuss externally linked attachments, which can be stored in the cloud.

All future exercises assume you have completed this installation.

---

[5] https://landing.mailerlite.com/webforms/landing/x2n4r0

STEP 1

Go to the <u>ZOTERO DOWNLOAD</u>[6] site.

STEP 2

For Windows users, click DOWNLOAD. For Mac, Linux, iOS, and other supported platforms, click OTHER PLATFORMS. Click the INSTALLATION HELP link for platform-specific instructions.

STEP 3

Go to your computer's DOWNLOADS folder and double-click on the Zotero setup program, which should be the most recent download. iOS tablet users will be redirected to app download instructions.

STEP 4

Your computer may ask you to allow the app to make changes. Click YES.

STEP 5

Follow the installation instructions on your device, accepting the default options unless you are an advanced user familiar with the choices.

STEP 6

Launch Zotero when the installation is complete.

WELCOME SCREEN

When set up for the first time, Zotero presents the WELCOME TO ZOTERO! screen. Once you begin to add things to your Zotero library, this screen will disappear—never appearing again, unless you create a new Zotero profile or delete all your data. Here is what I encourage you to do for each item at this stage:

---

[6] https://www.zotero.org/download/

*The WELCOME TO ZOTERO screen guides you to a few
essential setup items.*

QUICK START GUIDE

The QUICK START GUIDE link opens Zotero's documentation to the
basics. My book will supersede the material you find there as you
get your bearings. But later, when you have a quick question, this
guide can often give you a quick answer. Create a bookmark for
this page, so that you can find your way back. (Please note that
Zotero's documentation does not yet appear updated for Zotero 7.)

INSTALL ZOTERO CONNECTOR

The ZOTERO CONNECTOR plugin is one of Zotero's most valuable
features and the first thing that sold me on the product. It allows
you to import knowledge assets from online data sources like
WORLDCAT with the press of a button on your web browser. We
will talk about it in more detail in Chapter 5. Install the plugin
now, while you have Zotero's instructions at hand. If the ZOTERO
CONNECTOR download is not defaulting to your current browser,
click the SHOW ALL CONNECTORS link in the bottom-left of Zotero's

site to reveal links to other browser versions. If none of these browsers is your choice, see the text at the bottom of the page for other options to pull web information into Zotero.

Set Up Syncing

Syncing, if you desire to do it, requires you to set up a Zotero account. You can get a free account, and I strongly encourage you to use this feature. I will be walking you through this in the section titled Your Zotero Account and Syncing, later in this chapter. You do not need to do this now.

GETTING AROUND THE ZOTERO WORKSPACE

Zotero presents a simple workspace, with most of its content and features accessible on or within a click or two of the main window. The workspace begins as an essentially empty place called My Library, awaiting the contents you will add and the organizational structure you will create to hold the contents.

The main workspace includes four panes that can be repositioned, resized, or hidden when helpful. You will carry out most of your work in these interactive panes and the Zotero Reader. Choices you make in one pane affect what you see in the others.

Zotero's documentation does not typically name these panes, referring to them as the "left pane," "right pane," and so forth. Given that they can be repositioned, I prefer to label them functionally for our purposes here. The labels below correspond to the library functions the panes serve. My invented labels might not carry over when other writers are describing this interface, but they will give us a common language here.

The use of the various plugins available to extend Zotero's functions may change details in the workspace. A plugin might add a tab, menu, or new menu items. If you see an element in my illustrations that is missing from yours, it is likely because of a plugin. If you see something in your just-installed workspace that is missing from my illustrations, congratulations, the Zotero developers have added something new.

WORKSPACE PANES

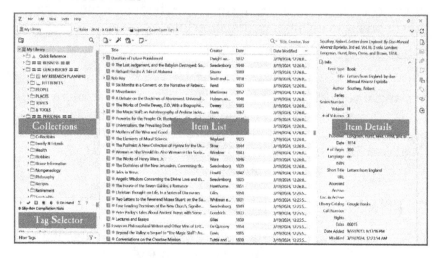

The bulk of Zotero's work is done in these four interactive panes and the ZOTERO READER, which appears in tabs behind it, when PDFs, HTML snapshots, or EPUB files are open.

COLLECTIONS

The COLLECTIONS pane displays your organizational structure. Here, you will decide how to group information to maximize its use in your research. You can create multiple layers of subcollections to control your collections further. In this book, I use the terms COLLECTION, SUBCOLLECTION, and FOLDER interchangeably. Zotero will allow you to nest folders inside of folders without limit.

ITEM LIST

The ITEM LIST pane serves much as the catalogs do in public libraries. It is your map to all the knowledge assets you have collected or created. The assets (Zotero calls them "items") displayed at any given time depend on what you have selected in the COLLECTIONS pane. At the top of COLLECTIONS, you will see MY LIBRARY. When you click on it, the ITEM LIST pane displays a master list of every knowledge asset you have documented. This allows you to search across all these items simultaneously or to sort or filter them by various criteria. This is the only pane you cannot collapse out of sight, though you can resize it and stack it on top of the ITEM DETAILS if preferred

ITEM DETAILS

The ITEM DETAILS pane holds the essential data of the Zotero database. Here, you gather information on each of your research items. Your item might be a single record, like a lone source reference entry or a note. Often items are gathered in a packet of notes, files, and links, attached to a reference item.

The ITEM DETAILS pane gathers a variety of information about each item, accessible using icons down the right side, and displayed in the following sections:

- INFO: This section gathers source reference information, with a changing set of fields based on your selected ITEM TYPE.

- ABSTRACT: This section holds a summary of the item.

- ATTACHMENTS: This section displays links to any files attached to the item. It displays a preview of the first or of a selected PDF, EPUB, HTML snapshot, or image among the attachments.

- NOTES: This section allows for the collection of textual information applicable to the item, and you can attach as many NOTES as you need.[7] If multiple NOTES have been added to a single reference, a list of them appears here until a NOTE is selected and fills the pane.

- LIBRARIES AND COLLECTIONS: This section displays any collections the selected item is in and the paths to the item.

- ANNOTATIONS: This section appears only when an attachment has been selected. It presents all annotations marked in the document.

---

[7] A remarkable plugin called BETTER NOTES allows you to create structured notes with its templates. If you have a standard form or report you want to use repeatedly, BETTER NOTES will support that. This guide will not give detail on plugins, except for the ones that are developed by Zotero. But another *Quick Guide* will describe them in detail.

- TAGS: This section allows you to assign tags that filter your items into predefined groups.

- RELATED: This section allows you to link your item and its notes to other items in your Zotero library.

- LOCATE: This button displays a menu of external resources that might be associated with the selected item in the ITEM LIST. The options are generated based on the type of item. Notes will not bring up a menu.

  - For source items and attachments, the first option is to OPEN PDF [SNAPSHOT/EPUB] IN NEW TAB. For PDFs and source items, an option to VIEW ONLINE will appear if the record contains a URL.

  - The LIBRARY LOOKUP option will attempt to retrieve the source from the catalog of a participating library you have set up in SETTINGS > GENERAL > LOCATE and are logged into. To set this up, the library must have made a "RESOLVER" path available.[8]

  - The GOOGLE SCHOLAR option allows you to search for the selected item on the Google Scholar website. It defaults at installation and is the first of what might become many LOOKUP ENGINE options. A future version of Zotero will include a user-friendly method to add other web search sources through the MANAGE LOOKUP ENGINES option.

This design allows space for additional sections to be added by plugins. The sections can be collapsed and expanded by clicking on the section headings or using the tools. To collapse or expand all sections simultaneously, right-click on a section heading for the option.

TAG SELECTOR

The TAG SELECTOR pane at the bottom-left corner of your Zotero workspace allows you to filter your ITEM LIST view to include only

---

[8] https://www.zotero.org/support/locate/openurl_resolvers

those items assigned a chosen tag. Tags are keywords, phrases, emojis, or symbols that connect a group of your items under common themes or statuses. You can also color code up to nine tags to connect similar items visually. You can use emojis or text symbols to flag items with pictures that have meaning to you.

TAILORING THE WORKSPACE

You can adjust the visual appearance of Zotero to optimize the workspace for your needs. Go to the VIEW menu to see the options you have. You might find that the various tasks you are performing are optimized by changing these settings. You can change them as often as you like.

VIEW MENU OPTIONS

LAYOUT

The STANDARD view is the default view, which presents the ITEM LIST and ITEM DETAILS side by side. The STACKED view places the ITEM LIST above the ITEM DETAILS, with both panes at a maximized width. The STACKED view is beneficial when you need to display extra fields in the ITEM LIST. The standard view displays more rows in the ITEM LIST and gives you a fuller view of the reference information in the ITEM INFO section. The LAYOUT menu also allows you to hide or show three of the four panes—the COLLECTIONS, ITEM DETAILS, and TAG SELECTOR. You can also resize the panes by positioning your cursor over the border between panes until a double-headed arrow appears, then clicking and dragging. (If you drag very close to an outer edge of the workspace, a pane may disappear. You can restore it through this LAYOUT menu or by dragging the outer border of the workspace.)

DENSITY

You may select to have your workspace displayed in either a COMPACT or a COMFORTABLE density. The COMFORTABLE format is the view that has been used in Zotero before Release 7. The COMPACT view, released with Zotero 7, allows you to see more text on the screen, with letters and rows closer together.

FONT SIZE

Six font size options allow you to decide how much Zotero information (other than NOTES) you can see at a time—and how easy it is to see. You can experiment by choosing BIGGER or SMALLER until you have the ideal size for your needs. The RESET option sets your workspace to the smallest font size.

NOTE FONT SIZE

Within any NOTE, you have substantial control over your font size. Choose an option in the drop-down list from size 11 to 96. A large size can be very helpful for those with vision challenges.

SYSTEM SETTINGS

We will be talking about various settings as we get into deeper discussions of features. For your reference, I offer here a quick overview of them, so that you will be aware of the sort of things that can be altered as you use Zotero. From the menu, choose EDIT > SETTINGS. The toolbar along the side allows you to set preferences in five different categories.

URGENT MESSAGE: If you are using the free version of Zotero, it is critical that you deselect two values in the SETTINGS before you begin your regular work. Both settings allow websites to send attachments to your Zotero database, rather than just reference information. If you are not ready to pay for Zotero storage, turn off these two flags under FILE HANDLING on the GENERAL tab:

○ Automatically attach associated PDFs and other files when saving items

○ Automatically take snapshots when creating items from web pages

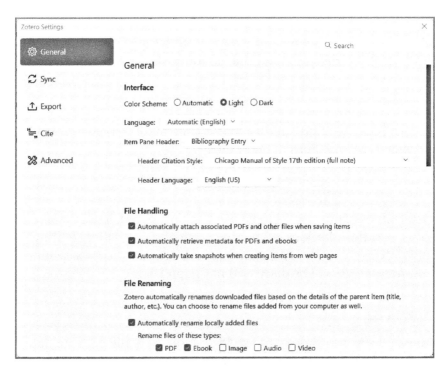

System settings are altered from the EDIT menu on the main toolbar. Some plugins will add items below the five categories on the left edge of the view.

MAIN SETTINGS

GENERAL

Sets your preferences for a light or dark screen or one automatically determined by your monitor's settings. Establishes how Zotero will handle materials imported, saved, named, viewed, attached, copied, and deleted. Sets language option. Allows university library users to "locate," connecting to their participating institution's library catalog. Choices made regarding the handling of PDFs, HTML snapshots, and EPUB books can impact the size of the database and might require a paid Zotero account. See more in Chapters 4, 7, and 9.

SYNC

Manages the syncing of your data to Zotero's available cloud storage, including choices about the handling of attachments.

EXPORT

Determines the nature and format of information to be exported or copied out of Zotero to other environments.

CITE

Determines citation style to be used, inclusion of URLs in citations, and the addition and modification of styles. Offers editing and preview of styles. Facilitates installation of word processing add-ons, which will be discussed in Chapter 8.

ADVANCED

Manages site translators and style updates. Sets the paths to data and attachment storage on the user's device, creates keyboard shortcuts, sets RSS feed defaults, and manages indexing. Offers HIDDEN SETTINGS for programming customization by advanced users. (Zotero cannot support user customizations).

―――――

Zotero's online documentation includes descriptions of all the listed settings, including some that we will not cover in this book. You can find them at SETTINGS.⁹ You will also see more options added to the SETTINGS as you install Zotero plugins like BETTER NOTES and ACTIONS AND TAGS FOR ZOTERO. Some plugins add settings options to the TOOLS menu.

―――――――――――――

⁹ https://www.zotero.org/support/preferences

SETTING UP YOUR ZOTERO SYSTEM

YOUR ZOTERO ACCOUNT AND SYNCING

You must establish an account to sync your data to Zotero's cloud for the first time. While syncing is optional, it is highly recommended for two reasons: (1) many users work on multiple computers and need access to the same data across all devices, and (2) eventually, your computer may fail or need to be replaced. Zotero's syncing mechanism allows your data to be stored and updated on multiple devices. Its cloud storage keeps a copy of your work, enabling you to quickly and easily restore it to a computer when needed or transfer your Zotero database to a new computer.

It's important to note that syncing is for convenience and utility, not for full data protection against all disasters. This service provides a constantly updated copy of your data, not a protected static backup. If your data becomes corrupted, the corrupted data will sync to Zotero's cloud immediately. Therefore, you should back up your data regularly to a secure location, preferably a cloud service that supports backups and allows you to keep multiple versions. For instance, I use AOMEI Backupper Standard to back up Zotero and other resources on my PC to Dropbox Plus, which retains versions of my backups for 30 days.

Zotero syncs text notes and reference data for free and provides 300 MB of free storage for syncing a small amount of stored attachment data. You can extend this storage by linking to attachments stored elsewhere rather than storing them directly in Zotero. However, there are benefits to keeping your materials entirely in Zotero (see Chapter 4). Zotero's storage options are reasonably priced if you choose to upgrade.

EXERCISE 2. ESTABLISH ACCOUNT AND START SYNCING

For our purposes now, I will assume you will start with the free storage option of Zotero. You can change this at any time. Here's how you set it up:

STEP 1

On the menu, choose EDIT > SETTINGS.

STEP 2

Click the SYNC button on the left-side toolbar to open the DATA SYNCING window.

STEP 3

Click CREATE ACCOUNT and follow Zotero's instructions to establish your account.

STEP 4

Return to the DATA SYNCING window, enter the USERNAME and PASSWORD set up in STEP 3, and click SET UP SYNCING.

STEP 5

Accept the defaults on the Zotero SETTING's SYNC panel for the moment. As we look at the choices related to attachments later, you might want to alter certain values.

RETRIEVING SAMPLE DATA

Zotero is easiest to learn with real data, especially when it is specifically chosen to highlight certain features. The following exercises use a sample dataset that you can download for free from my company's online store. If you purchased the book from my online store, this data was included with your download document, and you can start at Step 4.

EXERCISE 3. RETRIEVING SAMPLE DATA

Follow these instructions to retrieve your sample data and import it into your Zotero database.

STEP 1

Access the sample data product from Genohistory.com: SAMPLE DATA FOR A QUICK GUIDE TO ZOTERO 7.[10] Use the password QGZ7 (case-sensitive).

STEP 2

Click ADD TO CART, then VIEW CART. Ensure there is a $0 balance unless you have added something else. Click CHECKOUT.

STEP 3

At the time of this writing, my shop requires the billing name, address, and email fields to be completed, even when there is nothing to bill. I apologize for this inconvenience. Check the box labeled I AGREE TO THE WEBSITE TERMS AND CONDITIONS. Then click PLACE ORDER.

STEP 4

A receipt will appear with a large green button labeled "Z7-Sample-Data.zip." Click the button and a zipped file will download to your computer.

STEP 5

Go to the DOWNLOADS folder on your computer and right-click on the new zip file. Choose EXTRACT ALL and browse to where you want to place the sample data. The extracted folder should contain a single item: ZOTERO 7 QUICK GUIDE.RDF.

STEP 6

In Zotero, select your MY LIBRARY collection, and from the menu choose FILE > IMPORT. Select A FILE, then click NEXT. Locate the file you extracted and click OPEN. Choose COPY FILES TO THE ZOTERO STORAGE FOLDER and click NEXT. When it confirms that the items have been imported, click FINISH.

---

[10] https://genohistory.com/product/QGZ7-data/

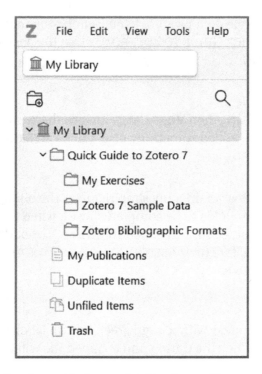

*A collection with three subcollections will appear with
sample data and format examples.*

You should now see a folder called QUICK GUIDE TO ZOTERO 7 in
your COLLECTIONS pane. Nested under this are three folders titled
MY EXERCISES, ZOTERO 7 SAMPLE DATA, and ZOTERO BIBLIO-
GRAPHIC FORMATS. If you do not see them, click on the arrow to
the left of the main folder to expand the contents.

DATA STORAGE ON YOUR COMPUTER

To determine where Zotero is storing your computer's copy of the
data by default, navigate to EDIT > SETTINGS > ADVANCED and locate the FILES AND FOLDERS section. The LINKED ATTACHMENT
BASE DIRECTORY will be discussed in Chapter 4. The DATA DIREC-
TORY LOCATION indicates where your Zotero data (excluding linked
attachments) is stored by default. If you choose to store attachments in your Zotero database rather than externally, these

attachments will be saved in subfolders of the STORAGE folder within your data directory. You can select a different location for your data storage, but ensure it is not in a folder synced to any cloud storage service other than Zotero's.

ZOTERO'S DATA SECURITY

Zotero is open-source software and does not secure your data on your computer with a password. If you share your computer login with others, your Zotero content will be accessible to them. If you do not share your computer, your Zotero data is as secure as your computer is from hackers and thieves. In any case, do not use Zotero to store passwords or credit card numbers.

You may separate your work into multiple Zotero profiles if that is helpful. For example, you can keep work-related Zotero information on your office computer and your home computer, while maintaining a personal Zotero library only on your home computer using SEPARATE PROFILES.[11] (A paid Zotero storage arrangement applies to only one profile.)

Regarding data synced to the Zotero cloud, great care is taken to protect your privacy. For more details, see the ZOTERO PRIVACY POLICY[12] and ZOTERO SECURITY[13] pages to understand how Zotero safeguards your stored data.

IMPORTANT NOTE: Using Zotero's paid storage does not mean your data exists only there. The primary database of your research resides on your hard drive. Zotero stores a *copy* of your data, continually updated, on its web servers to facilitate syncing between computers and to provide access to a copy wherever you go.

GETTING HELP

If you have questions about this book and its exercises or about applying Zotero to history or genealogy, you are encouraged to

---

[11] https://www.zotero.org/support/kb/multiple_profiles
[12] https://www.zotero.org/support/privacy
[13] https://www.zotero.org/support/security

post them on the GENOHISTORY FORUM.[14] Or you can use the GENOHISTORY CONTACT FORM[15] to send me a private message.

My counsel when encountering problems will always start with these instructions:

1. DOCUMENT THE ISSUE: Immediately take note of where you were in the system and what you were doing when the problem occurred. Keep detailed notes as you proceed through the following steps.

2. UPDATE ZOTERO: Ensure you are using the latest version of Zotero. If not, load the newest version and see if the problem persists.

3. RESTART ZOTERO: Exit Zotero and reopen it. Does the problem persist?

4. TROUBLESHOOT PLUGINS: From the HELP menu, choose RE-START IN TROUBLESHOOTING MODE. Zotero will temporarily disable all your plugins, close itself, then reopen. If the problem persists, enable the plugins one by one, testing after each. If you identify the problematic plugin, report it to the developer. Go to TOOLS > PLUGINS and click on the plugin name to find the developer's homepage. If the plugins don't seem related to your issue, proceed to the next step.

5. REBOOT YOUR COMPUTER: Does the problem still occur?

6. USE ZOTERO'S HELP OPTIONS: Keep the notes you took. If you need to seek help from the ZOTERO FORUM, you can report what you have already done, saving time.

ZOTERO'S HELP OPTIONS

Zotero provides multiple resources to help you answer questions or solve problems. All these support features are accessible through the HELP menu.

---

[14] https://genohistory.com/forum
[15] https://genohistory.com/contact/

SUPPORT AND DOCUMENTATION

Zotero's online documentation covers the essentials of using the software, though it appears as of this writing that it has not yet been fully updated to reflect version 7 changes. You can find helpful information in the KNOWLEDGE BASE[16] and FREQUENTLY ASKED QUESTIONS[17] sections.

TROUBLESHOOTING INFORMATION

The GETTING HELP[18] page on Zotero's website guides you through troubleshooting steps before escalating an issue to the public forum. It ensures you are using the latest version of the software and provides reports on known issues.

DISCUSSION FORUMS

Zotero's public discussion forum offers direct access to developers and a supportive community. Unlike most software development enterprises, Zotero allows you to interact directly with developers. Before posting a question, search the existing forum discussions and documentation for answers. The forums can bring quick resolutions. You will need your Zotero login to post messages. This direct access to developers also allows you to suggest new features.

REPORT ERRORS

If Zotero generates an error, select REPORT ERRORS from the HELP menu, follow the prompts, and send the error to Zotero for investigation. Be sure to describe the issue and detail your system setup, including the operating system and version.

UPDATING YOUR ZOTERO SOFTWARE

By default, Zotero routinely checks for software updates. If a new version is available, you will be notified the next time you open

---

[16] https://zotero.org/support/kb
[17] https://www.zotero.org/support/frequently_asked_questions
[18] https://www.zotero.org/support/getting_help

Zotero. To manually check for updates during a session, click CHECK FOR UPDATES on the HELP menu. For details on new features or fixes, visit the ZOTERO VERSION HISTORY[19] page. Updates are also posted on the GENOHISTORY FACEBOOK[20] page.

* * *

These resources ensure that you have comprehensive support while using Zotero, making it easier to resolve any issues and stay updated with the latest features.

---

[19] https://www.zotero.org/support/changelog
[20] https://www.facebook.com/genohistory

2. MANAGING KNOWLEDGE ASSETS

Knowledge management begins with the effective gathering of information. Zotero offers a robust framework for storing and organizing this information, ensuring it is readily accessible to researchers. This chapter introduces Zotero's comprehensive information-gathering system, detailing its tools and methods for citing sources, taking notes, and connecting related information to create valuable knowledge assets. All other features in Zotero build upon this essential foundation.

CHOOSING YOUR REFERENCE STYLE

Researchers must declare the sources of their information. Zotero aids in recording essential source reference information and generates properly formatted citations based on your chosen citation style. Students often follow specific styles assigned by their instructors, while scholars preparing for publication must adhere to their publisher's style guidelines. Each scholarly field typically has its preferred citation styles, and in the absence of other requirements, you should use the standard for your field.

Zotero supports thousands of citation styles, continuously expanding to meet the needs of various scholarly fields, subspecialties, and publishing environments. In the U.S., humanities fields, including history, often favor *The Chicago Manual of Style (CMOS)*, which is also widely accepted in genealogy.

You can switch between citation styles, though some data optimized for one style may not perfectly translate to another. For example, one style might require the country name for a publisher's location, while another might only need the city and state for U.S. cities. It is recommended to set up Zotero to use the style most common in your field and location. Always gather more information than you think you need to be prepared if a publisher requires a different style. You can change the citation style in your word processor's Zotero plugin (see Chapter 8) without altering Zotero's data.

To set your default citation style, select EDIT > SETTINGS and choose CITE from the toolbar. For our examples, we will use THE CHICAGO MANUAL OF STYLE 17TH EDITION (FULL NOTE). Select your

preferred style and check the box to INCLUDE URLS OF PAPER ARTI-
CLES IN REFERENCES (you can later deselect this if you do not want
lengthy URLs in your citations). Then, click OK to return to the
main window.

VIEWING THE ITEM LIST

Review your ITEM LIST to understand how Zotero structures and
displays the titles of the knowledge assets it refers to as "items." In
the COLLECTIONS pane to the left, click on the ZOTERO 7 SAMPLE
DATA folder. A set of reference items will appear in the ITEM LIST
pane.

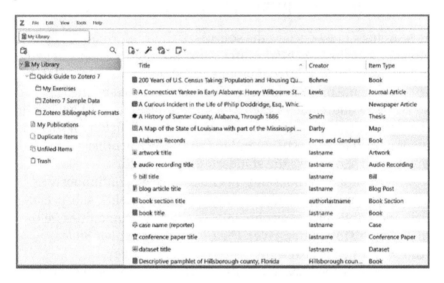

Sample data will appear in your ITEM LIST when you
select the sample folder you imported into MY LIBRARY.

In the ITEM LIST, you will notice a set of icons to the left of each
source record, representing the type of source. For example, a
book icon appears next to books, and a graduation cap icon appears beside dissertations. Zotero guides you in gathering the necessary information for source references based on the ITEM TYPE
you assign to a source.

Click on your sample items one by one and observe what appears in the ITEM DETAILS on the right. The first field in the INFO
section of the ITEM DETAILS is the ITEM TYPE, indicating the type of

source reference you are viewing. Zotero then displays the relevant fields for that reference type. Typically, you will not use all the fields, as some are specific to different citation styles.

While this book does not cover every potential item, type, and field, the following sections will describe core concepts. Most fields are self-explanatory. For information about altering the ITEM LIST view, see CHOOSING AND CONTROLLING COLUMNS in Chapter 6.

CREATING AN ITEM

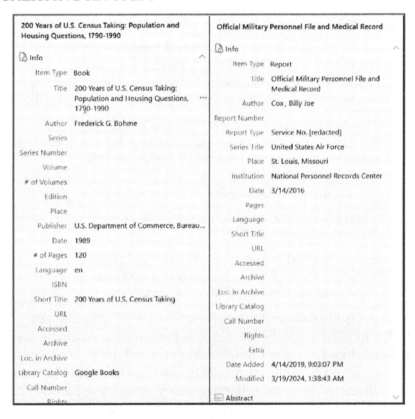

The ITEM TYPE you choose determines the available fields.
This shows two different views of the ITEM DETAILS, a
book (left) and a report (right).

Zotero includes a feature called ZOTERO CONNECTOR that simplifies the process of entering items. However, before learning this shortcut (Chapter 5), it is important to understand how to manually enter an item.

To manually enter a new item, click on the NEW ITEM button, the first icon on the toolbar above the ITEM LIST. From its dropdown menu, choose the item type for the reference you are creating. Depending on the type you choose, the INFO section will display a curated set of fields. For example, the illustration below shows a BOOK type on the left and a REPORT type on the right. While some fields are shared, others, like the book's ISBN or the report's INSTITUTION, are unique to their specific item types.

Some fields appear but are not included in citations or bibliographic references. The dates added and modified, for example, are at the bottom of the ITEM DETAILS and useful for your reference but are not used in the footnotes of an article or book. In *CMOS* style, the book's bibliographic data is formatted as follows:

Bohme, Frederick G. *200 Years of U.S. Census Taking: Population and Housing Questions, 1790–1990*. Washington, D.C.: U.S. Department of Commerce, Bureau of the Census, 1989. https://www.google.com/books/edition/200_Years_of_U_S_C ensus_Taking/uzmJpqoicHIC.

A military personnel record, cited with the REPORT item type, yields this reference in *CMOS* format:

Cox, Billy Joe. "Official Military Personnel File and Medical Record." Service No. [redacted]. United States Air Force. St. Louis, Missouri: National Personnel Records Center, March 14, 2016.

As you build data in Zotero, the software will minimize keystrokes by offering drop-down lists of previously used entries in certain fields. The author, publisher, and place fields, among others, will use type-ahead functionality based on your initial letters.

While many fields are self-explanatory, some have hidden or less obvious features. The most important ones are described in the following sections.

TITLES

Zotero's TITLE field can accommodate very long text strings, but not all of it may be carried over when your source is formatted as a citation in a formal paper.

The title, when output as a reference or citation, will adopt the format established by your chosen style. Normally, this will be what you want. Occasionally, however, your specific source may present challenges to the standard format.

You may find yourself creating a title for an untitled source or adding text to an existing title as a reminder that the article is a book review. I recommend enclosing any text not created by the original author in brackets. The brackets serve as a reminder that you might need to rework the title and its formatting when preparing a formal work for publication.

For example, you might have a title of an article that references a book, such as "Introduction to *The Confessions of Nat Turner*." Zotero, using CMOS style, is designed to put an article title in Roman type inside quotation marks. However, in this case, the title should be a mix of italic and Roman characters when properly formatted for publication.

While Zotero's TITLE field is not a full-blown rich-text field, you can handle such situations using basic HTML tags if you are familiar with them. For instance, to format the title properly in your bibliography, enter it in the TITLE field as: INTRODUCTION TO <i>THE CONFESSIONS OF NAT TURNER</i>, which italicizes everything between the two HTML markers. Using "b" where the "i" characters are will make the enclosed text bold, if you have a need for that.

Additionally, some reference items brought in automatically—through the ZOTERO CONNECTOR or other methods discussed in this chapter and the next—may not format the title as you prefer. You can convert a title to sentence case (only the first letter capitalized) or title case (first letter and proper nouns capitalized) using an automated tool. These options appear in the right-click menu when you right-click on the TITLE field. If you first left-click into the TITLE field and then right-click, the options will not appear.

By following these guidelines, you can ensure that your titles are accurately formatted for your citations and references.

SHORT TITLE

Many reference and citation styles, including *CMOS*, require the second and subsequent citations of a source within a chapter to be in a shortened version. The SHORT TITLE field allows you to choose how that version will appear.

AUTHORS, EDITORS, AND OTHER ITEM CREATORS

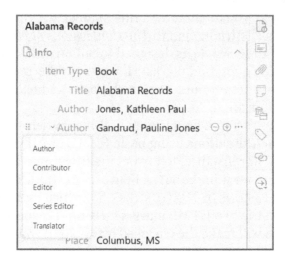

Zotero allows multiple authors, editors, or other participants for a source record.

Creators take on different roles and labels depending on the ITEM TYPE. For a BOOK item type, you can change creator roles and add collaborators by clicking the small arrow to the left of the AUTHOR field. Available creator roles include AUTHOR, CONTRIBUTOR, EDITOR, SERIES EDITOR, and TRANSLATOR. For a BOOK SECTION item type, you have both an AUTHOR and a BOOK AUTHOR option, allowing you to note a section authored by someone other than the book's main authors or editors.

The dotted icon to the left of a creator's line also allows you to rearrange the order of multiple contributors, which will affect their display in your formal citations. The PLUS and MINUS buttons to the right of the names allow you to add or remove contributors. In the example above, you have coauthors Jones and Gandrud. The small rectangle to the left of the MINUS button (not shown here) lets you enter the creator names as one field or two.

Zotero uses the roles you choose for creators in various item types to generate the correct CMOS format for that type of citation. For an INTERVIEW item type, for example, Zotero offers creator roles such as INTERVIEW WITH, CONTRIBUTOR, INTERVIEWER, and TRANSLATOR. The INTERVIEW WITH person will be the key creator, and Zotero will insert "interview by" followed by the interviewer's name, as the style recommends.

An interview with Michelle Obama by Oprah Winfrey on NBC News would be formatted like this:

Obama, Michelle. *Former first lady Michelle Obama describes life in the White House.* Interview by Oprah Winfrey. Television, November 14, 2018. https://www.nbcnews.com/video/oprah-interviews-former-first-lady-michelle-obama-1370056771738.

The INTERVIEW item type offers creator roles of INTERVIEWER, INTERVIEW WITH, and others.

To record a LETTER item type, you will need to designate both an AUTHOR and a RECIPIENT, along with the date, which will appear like this in the bibliography:

Mayberry, J.D. Letter to H.D. Clayton, February 22, 1886. Acumen - The University of Alabama Libraries' Digital Archives. William

Stanley Hoole Special Collections Library. https://digitalcollections.libraries.ua.edu/digital/collection/u0003_0000313/id/6872/rec/1.

Generally, there will be no official title on a letter for citation notes. Zotero will fill in a bracketed placeholder in the ITEM LIST. In this case, the title appears as "[Letter to Clayton]."

Many variations of the CREATOR role are available, depending on the ITEM TYPE. Some are usable in citations, but some are purely for your reference. To see the latest list and their citation-readiness, visit ZOTERO ITEM TYPES AND FIELDS: ITEM CREATORS[1] in Zotero's online documentation.

QUICK TIP: If a creator's first and last name have accidentally been entered in reverse, right-click on the name field and choose SWAP FIRST/LAST. You can also fix the capitalization case using the right-click menu.

DATE FORMATS

Date	1858-04-17	y m d
Date	16 December 1823	d m y

Zotero interprets all dates behind the scenes into a form for proper sorting.

You may enter a date in one of numerous standard formats, and Zotero will interpret it, as needed. The letters to the right of the item's date reveal the interpretation Zotero has made. In the first case, the date was entered in a year-month-day (y m d) arrangement. The second was formatted with day-month-year (d m y).

While these dates would sort badly in alphanumeric order, Zotero knows how to convert the dates behind the scenes, sorting them in proper chronological order. In the next image, you see the ITEM LIST of your sample data sorted in date order, despite the various date formats used.

---

[1] https://www.zotero.org/support/kb/item_types_and_fields#item_creators

While Zotero will allow you to type random text or date ranges into the date field, it cannot include them in a citation. It will assume that the last episode of four digits that appears anywhere in the date field is the year. It will treat it as a year in the citation. You may get creative with data entry in many Zotero fields, but this needs to be a specific day, month, or year.

Title	Creator	Item Type	Date
A Map of the State of Louisiana with ...	Darby	Map	1816
A Curious Incident in the Life of Philip...		Newspaper Article	1844-03-16
The Mormons		Magazine Article	March 1851
Descriptive pamphlet of Hillsborough...	Hillsborough co...	Book	1885
U.S. Reports: Fletcher v. Fuller, 120 U....	United States--S...	Statute	1886
[Letter to Clayton]	Mayberry	Letter	22 Feb 1886
[Paragraph of a letter from the royal o...	Griffin	Journal Article	1891-06-01
The 151st Field Artillery Brigade	Russell	Book	1919
Map of Portion of Louisiana—Vicinity ...		Map	1920
Alabama Records	Jones and Gand...	Book	1980
A History of Sumter County, Alabama,...	Smith	Thesis	1988
200 Years of U.S. Census Taking: Popul...	Bohme	Book	1989
A Connecticut Yankee in Early Alabam...	Lewis	Journal Article	2006-04
Nott, Josiah Clark	Horsman	Dictionary Entry	2013-01-02
Official Military Personnel File and Me...	Cox	Report	3/14/2016
Transcribing historical manuscripts in ...	Baker	Blog Post	2016-07-13
Photograph of Margarette A Carnath...		Artwork	2016-12-10
Passenger Record — Maggie Carnath...		Document	2016-12-12 02:32:45

Zotero can interpret valid date formats and will sort
various formats into proper date order.

QUICK TIP: In a limited departure from the no-random-text rule, you can type "yesterday," "today," or "tomorrow" in a date field to retrieve those dates.

URL

The URL field in the item's INFO tab will be included in a citation or bibliographic output if you have set your style to include it in the CITE tab of your SYSTEM SETTINGS. A URL address can be attached to an item, instead, if you want to capture it, but do not want it to be in a citation. You can access the website by double-clicking on the item in the ITEM LIST or clicking on the GO TO icon to the upper-right of the URL.

THE DATE ADDED AND MODIFIED FIELDS

Zotero saves data each time you exit a field and applies the DATE ADDED and MODIFIED fields to each item for your reference. The DATE ADDED field remains constant, indicating when you first captured the source, while the MODIFIED field updates to show the last time you made any changes to the item.

Zotero also tracks these dates for notes and attachments. To view these dates, you can either select the GENERATE REPORT FROM ITEM option from the right-click menu or add the date fields to your ITEM LIST view.

If you want to manually maintain a complete record of every time you consulted a source—what genealogists call a RESEARCH LOG—you can use the notes feature to capture relevant details. Alternatively, you can attach a log file using a word processing document or spreadsheet. An efficient way to achieve this is by attaching a new child note each time you revisit a source. Each child note will have an automatic timestamp in the DATE ADDED field.

IMPORTANT NOTE: If you export Zotero data and import it elsewhere, these dates will be reset to the date the information is added to the new location.

THE EXTRA FIELD

Citation and reference requirements continually evolve as scholarly fields and research projects change. The EXTRA field in Zotero provides a flexible way to adapt to these evolving needs, especially for requirements that are not yet universally recognized by the user base. When multiple users need Zotero to accommodate changing standards in their research areas, the development team considers using specific labels in the EXTRA field to bridge the gap.

For example, historians can use the label "Original Date" followed by a colon and a year to indicate both the new publication date of a classic book and its original year of publication. This approach requires the user to know the specific label to use, but it allows Zotero to reflect unique or emerging citation requirements.

Some users with CSL (CITATION STYLE LANGUAGE) knowledge create variations of a reference style and use the EXTRA field to add desired fields. Zotero's documentation describes how to create your a style variation at EDITING CSL STYLES—STEP-BY-STEP GUIDE.[2] If you create your own style, you will be responsible for revising it when Zotero's database changes impact it.

If you choose to display your EXTRA field in the ITEM LIST, it will display whatever is at the top of the field. Therefore, if there is something you want to see in your ITEM LIST or to sort by, it needs to be the first thing you put into EXTRA.

You may also use the EXTRA field to hold data that is of use to you. It can be notes specific to your research. The important consideration, though, is to avoid using text that could later be mistaken by Zotero's software as a supplemental text to alter a citation.

Zotero's documentation describes the EXTRA field and its currently available supplemental options at ZOTERO ITEM TYPES AND FIELDS.[3]

QUICK TIP: Get into the habit of right-clicking on everything in Zotero. Many useful tools are embedded in these context-sensitive menus, and often roll out as a tasty surprise in what looks otherwise like a minor unrelated update between major releases.

EXERCISE 4. ADD A BOOK

In this exercise and the next, we will add the same book in two different ways and with varying outcomes. We will start with a manual entry.

---

[2] https://www.zotero.org/support/dev/citation_styles/style_ editing_step-by-step

[3] https://www.zotero.org/support/kb/item_types_and_fields

STEP 1

Click on the MY EXERCISES collection (left pane) to select where your new book item will be stored. Then click the NEW ITEM button on your toolbar. Select BOOK from the drop-down list. (If it does not appear, click MORE, and choose it from the submenu.) A new item with the BOOK item type will appear in the ITEM DETAILS.

STEP 2

In the TITLE field, type: "The Elements of Style (test)." Tab out of the field to save the title value.

STEP 3

Enter "Strunk Jr." in the AUTHOR (last) field, tab over, and type "William" in the AUTHOR (first) field. (If there is only one field, type "William Strunk Jr.")

STEP 4

Click the PLUS SIGN button to the right of William's name to create a new author line. Fill in the last name "White" and the first name "E. B."

STEP 5

Move down and type "4" in the EDITION field; "Boston" in PLACE; "Pearson" in PUBLISHER; and "1999" in DATE. Tab out of the field to save the data.

QUICK DATA ENTRY OPTIONS

ADD ITEM(S) BY IDENTIFIER

Zotero allows you to automate data entry if you have standard identifiers for your sources. On the main workspace toolbar, the ADD ITEM(S) BY IDENTIFIER button provides this shortcut. By entering a book's International Standard Book Number (ISBN), a digital resource's Digital Object Identifier (DOI), or several other types of identifiers, Zotero will automatically pull the relevant information into a new source item.

The accuracy of the data depends on the diligence of the person who entered the bibliographic reference into the external databases Zotero consults. Therefore, it is important to verify that the information has been correctly imported and make any necessary corrections.

EXERCISE 5. ADD BOOK USING ISBN

STEP 1

Click on ADD ITEM(S) BY IDENTIFIER (second on the toolbar above the ITEM LIST) and type the following ISBN into the field: 9780205309023.

STEP 2

Press ENTER. That's it! You have added the book.

You should now have two copies of the 4th edition of Strunk and White's *Elements of Style* in your MY EXERCISES collection. Click on each one to view the data in your ITEM DETAILS. Assuming nothing has changed in the world's library information or "metadata" since the writing of this book, you will notice that this second method pulled in substantially more information than we typed in the manual record, including a publication year.

STEP 3 (BONUS STEP)

Right-click on the TITLE and choose TITLE CASE. The words "The elements of style" should now be converted to "The Elements of Style."

The new book has a substantial abstract and tells us where the information came from: Amazon. It has also attached a link containing the URL of this item in Amazon's store. It might appear as a simple arrowhead to the left of the item in the ITEM LIST. Click on that and the attached link will appear.

SNEAK PREVIEW OF THE ZOTERO CONNECTOR

If you are adding a reference item to Zotero from a book in your hand, the option above works very well. However, I find myself much more often extracting source information from online tools, like WORLDCAT.ORG, a local library's online catalog, or even Amazon. In Chapter 5, I will introduce you to the feature that first sold me on Zotero as my must-have tool for graduate school. The ZOTERO CONNECTOR allows you to create a robust Zotero reference record with only one click.

ADDING NOTES

You can create as many notes as you want for any given reference item in Zotero. As you add notes, they will appear in a list under the NOTES tab in the ITEM DETAILS. To create a new note for an existing item, either click ADD in the NOTES tab or right-click on the item in the ITEM LIST and select ADD NOTE.

You can also create standalone notes in your ITEM LIST. These can be used for various types of information that are not connected to a specific source reference but are useful to you—such as thoughts, ideas, to-do lists, or reminders.

When you type a new note, the first line will be treated as the note's title. Substantial text can fit into any note—more than 400,000 plain-text characters in my last experiment, almost three times the length of this book. However, keep in mind that Zotero will sync any item that has had a change. If you frequently update a large note, it may result in slower syncing. Splitting your material into multiple notes is usually a better alternative for lengthy text, as Zotero will only sync the parts that have changed since the last sync.

Another type of note, called "annotation notes," will be discussed in Chapter 7. These notes are connected to an attachment rather than to its parent item in the ITEM LIST. Annotation notes and regular notes are effectively integrated with a plugin called BETTER NOTES, which will be described in depth in a future Quick Guide. This plugin allows you to create master notes that integrate fragments of thought from multiple other notes.

Notes Formatting Tools

Notes are enabled for rich text, MARKDOWN, and HTML formatting. See a document titled MARKDOWN FORMATTING FOR ZOTERO NOTES in your sample data for information on how MARKDOWN can speed up the formatting of notes. The icons on the NOTES toolbar offer the following functions for child and standalone notes:

Displays the formatting options for bold, italics, underlined, strikethrough, subscript, superscript, and monospaced text. Offers the following paragraph styles: Heading 1, Heading 2, Heading 3, Paragraph, Monospaced, Bulleted List, Numbered List, Block Quote, and Math Block.

Alters text colors to one of eight options other than the standard black. If a color has been applied and you wish to return to black, use the Tx tool below to remove the formatting.

Highlights the selected text with one of eight colors. If a color has been applied and you wish to return to unhighlighted text, use the Tx tool below to remove the formatting.

Clears text formatting to the selected text. It does not clear monospaced, bulleted, numbered, block quoted, or math blocks. These can be toggled off with the same tool that turned them on, or they can be deleted.

Creates a hyperlink. Links in Zotero notes, when clicked directly, will present a second link to be clicked. If you hold your control key while clicking, it goes directly to the referenced site. If a previously linked site is already open in the background, the link might open out of sight in the already open browser.

Opens the Zotero selection bar for creating citations and references within the note, just as it does in word processing software with the Zotero add-on described in Chapter 8.

Opens find-and-replace operations within the note.

Opens to a menu of options for notes:

- EDIT IN A SEPARATE WINDOW allows you to create a display of the current note in a separate window, which can be resized and positioned as needed.

- Notes-related plugins and future notes features will be added to this menu.

CONTEXT-SENSITIVE FORMATTING

More functions are available from your right-click menu when your cursor is within a note. The CUT, COPY, and PASTE options can be activated by the standard shortcuts. It offers the RIGHT-TO-LEFT option for languages with that requirement. You can align a paragraph to the right, center, or left of the pane. You can insert an image, table, or math equation. This menu allows you to run a spell check on the contents of this specific note. And finally, the LANGUAGES option allows you to choose the language of your notes dictionary.

QUICK TIP: You can drag and drop (QUICK COPY) a note into another word processing tool like Word, Google Docs, a PC's default notepad app, or WordPad. Make sure your other tool's text window is visible in the background. Click on the note in your ITEM LIST pane, drag, and drop it into the word processing tool. Or you can highlight a portion or all the text within the note and drag and drop it to the desired place.

EDIT NOTES IN SEPARATE WINDOWS

Zotero is not technically a windows-oriented program. But much of our work is in notes, which can be opened in independent windows. You can size and place them wherever they serve your work. This can be particularly helpful when you need to take notes while consulting something in another window. You can narrow the note window beside the window from which you are extracting, or to which you are adding, information.

Notes can be popped out of the larger workspace into separate windows by double-clicking on the note in the ITEM LIST. Or click on the triple-dot icon in the toolbar above the note and select EDIT IN A SEPARATE WINDOW. You may also open multiple windows and position them all beside each other when you want to consider some ideas in juxtaposition or contrast.

QUICK TIP: Another way to simulate a multi-windowed environment is to use the WEB LIBRARY on Zotero's website. Log into your account at ZOTERO.ORG, and the WEB LIBRARY link is the first item on your menu. Though it does not have all the desktop software features, you can see and edit your data. You can open copies of your library in multiple browser windows.

ASSIGNING TAGS

Tags are a mechanism to group or flag your items in a meaningful way. Tags are often equivalent to a library's subject heading catalog, connecting items around a theme. They can also be used to flag the status of an item, letting you know which of your items you have on hand, for example, or which you have not yet read. You may use text, emojis, or a combination of the two to make the tag meaningful for your purposes. Some researchers prefer to use tags rather than collections to group similar items.

The TAG SELECTOR pane in the bottom-left corner of your main workspace allows you to display every item in a selected collection that has been assigned a particular tag. You can select multiple tags to narrow down a selection to items that have all the assigned tags.

You may assign any tag that is of use to you, in much the same way that you add notes. Click on the TAGS beside the ITEM DETAILS and click the plus sign (+) in the TAGS line. Once you have created a tag for use on an item, it will become available on any other items from a drop-down list that will appear when you type the first letter or two of the tag name. Once a tag exists in the system, you can also assign it to an item by dragging the item's entry from the ITEM LIST and dropping it on top of the tag in the TAG SELEC-TOR pane. You can delete or rename a tag by right-clicking on it in the TAG SELECTOR pane and choosing either DELETE or RENAME.

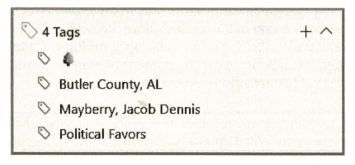

Tags can be emojis, symbols, text, or a blend of the two.
The tree emoji tells me this information needs to be
updated in my ancestor's family tree profile. The other
tags tie this item to a person, place, and theme.

QUICK TIP: If you enter multiple tags for an item, you can type each one and click SHIFT > ENTER. This creates a list. Click ADD after the last term, and each line will become a tag.

Some tags are inserted automatically from other sources. As you import items using ZOTERO CONNECTOR (see Chapter 5), they might come with AUTOMATIC TAGS already created—often the subject heading metadata created by libraries. If you prefer not to have these tags applied automatically, go to SETTINGS > GENERAL, under the MISCELLANEOUS heading. Deselect AUTOMATICALLY TAG ITEMS WITH KEYWORDS AND SUBJECT HEADINGS.

If you choose to keep the AUTOMATIC TAGS, there will be times that they come through with several terms together, separated by a punctuation symbol. Assuming there is a consistent character between the terms, Zotero can split the pieces into individual tags. Right-click on the tag and choose SPLIT.... Type the character that separates the terms, and Zotero will show you what the terms will look like. If there is one you do not want to keep, you can deselect it. If the terms are not labeled exactly as you would like, you can go ahead with the split, and then rename the new tags.

Up to nine tags can be color-coded, placing the color in a small square beside the item in the ITEM LIST. To color-code a tag, right-click on it in the TAG SELECTOR pane and choose ASSIGN COLOR.... You can choose a number between 1 and 9 to serve as your shortcut to apply the tag and its color to selected items in your ITEM LIST. With Zotero 7, an emoji as the first character in a tag will also appear beside your item in the ITEM LIST.

QUICK TIP: Zotero has an ingenious method for turning a tag into a status flag using emojis and color coding. You can use some or all your allotted color-coded tags to display emoji symbols, rather than the color block. A checkmark emoji could flag an item as finished. A lightning bolt could tell you an item needs to be handled quickly. A tree can tell a genealogist that this information needs to be updated in family tree software. See Chapter 3's "Emojis and Symbols" section for more information.

CONNECTING RELATED ITEMS

The RELATED tab allows you to connect a set of items that you want to recall together. For example, you might relate books in a series or multiple volumes. You might link a book with all the review articles you have collected about it. Genealogists have many reasons to connect items—creating family connections or tying all the probate records together for the processing of an ancestor's estate. You can link as many related items as you need and easily remove them by clicking the MINUS sign to the right.

You can add RELATED links in the same way you add tags and notes. Click the RELATED tab in your ITEM DETAILS, then click ADD. Find the item you want to flag as related. After creating this link,

the second record will show the link in its RELATED tab, also. Clicking on the link will take you to the related item.

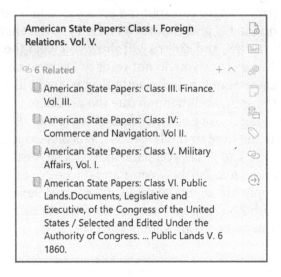

The RELATED tab allows you to group items with a
connection, like these volumes of the same set of federal
papers, all related to the Class I volume in the ITEM LIST.

QUICK TIP: You may also relate items or create hyperlinks between
items using the plugin called ACTIONS AND TAGS FOR ZOTERO. It
can automatically relate a block of items. This tool will be described in-depth in a future Quick Guide.

DELETING AND RESTORING ITEMS

To delete an item and any dependent items, right-click on it in the
ITEM LIST and choose MOVE ITEM TO TRASH. You can delete a de-
pendent item exclusively in the same way. The item(s) will no
longer appear in the ITEM LIST but will remain available in
Zotero's TRASH bin for a period of days designated in SETTINGS >
GENERAL in the MISCELLANEOUS section.

Zotero's TRASH can be found toward the bottom of the MY LI-
BRARY (upper) section of your COLLECTIONS pane. You will not

likely need to access it frequently but might occasionally need to manually delete something or restore something accidentally deleted.

When you click on the TRASH, all the items slated for removal will appear in your ITEM LIST. If the deleted item is an attachment or note in an item, the entire item will appear, but only the item to be deleted will appear in regular text format. All other items in that item, including the main reference, will be dimmed out and will not be deleted.

If you want to recover one of the trash items back to active use in your library, right-click on the specific item and choose RESTORE TO LIBRARY. The item will be available again for use. If you want to permanently delete one of the items, without emptying the entire trash bin, right-click on the item and click DELETE ITEM. To empty the TRASH completely, right-click on the TRASH collection and choose EMPTY TRASH.

The data in TRASH counts against any storage limits you have in the Zotero cloud. If you have deleted items to free up space, you must empty the TRASH and sync to fully free up the space.

EXERCISE 6. COMPLETING AND DELETING AN ITEM

PREREQUISITE: EXERCISE 3, 4, AND 5

This exercise will work with the book items you created, applying the various functions described in Chapter 2. If you have already experimented with the tools in the ITEM DETAILS tabs, this exercise will not be a prerequisite for other exercises. It can be skipped.

STEP 1

Click on MY EXERCISES in the COLLECTIONS pane. You should have two books. Select the one that has (test) at the end of the title.

STEP 2

Right-click on the chosen book and click ADD NOTE. In the new note, type "Sample Note." Click on the Aa tool and choose "Heading 1." The words should now be bold and larger.

STEP 3

Press ENTER and type "Genohistory." Select the word and click on
the INSERT LINK tool on the toolbar. To the "https://" that already
appears, add "genohistory.com" with no spaces. Click the
checkmark to set the link. Click back into the note. You'll now have
an active link called GENOHISTORY in the body of your note, which
will take you to my website.

STEP 4

Select the note's contents (CTRL+A). Right-click and choose ALIGN
> ALIGN CENTER and experiment with any more of the formatting
tools (1st four) on the toolbar.

STEP 5

Place your cursor after GENOHISTORY and press ENTER to create a
new line. Press [+] on the toolbar. In the red-outlined bar that appears, type "200 years." Select the book that appears, titled *200
Years of U.S. Census Taking: Population and Housing Questions,
1790–1990*, and press ENTER twice. A short in-text citation containing the text (Bohme, 1989) is added to the note. Click on the
same Strunk & White *Elements of Style* book in your ITEM LIST
again. A note labeled SAMPLE NOTE should now be a child item beneath the book's main record.

STEP 6

Delete the SAMPLE NOTE in this way: Select the NOTES tab in the
ITEM DETAILS. Click on the minus sign (-) in a circle to the right of
that note. Answer "OK" to the confirmation message.

STEP 7

Click on the RELATED tab, then click ADD to relate this book to the
other one we created. You probably have the MY EXERCISES collection active, and just the two *Elements of Style* books showing.
Click on the other version of the book (without TEST on the end)
and click OK. This title should now appear in your RELATED tab.

STEP 8

Click on the new RELATED item, and you will be instantly taken to the related book's record—which now shows the test book's title in its RELATED tab. (If you keep clicking on the related title, you will see that the ITEM LIST is moving its focus from one book to the other.) This will mean a lot more to you when these titles are scattered far apart, separated by thousands of records.

STEP 9

Click back on the INFO tab then click on the test book in the ITEM LIST. Right-click on it and choose MOVE ITEM TO TRASH. Click OK to confirm this decision.

STEP 10

In the COLLECTIONS pane, choose TRASH, which should be at the bottom of the available collections. Right-click on the test title and choose DELETE PERMANENTLY. Answer OK to confirm.

3. ORGANIZING RESEARCH COLLECTIONS

USING ZOTERO COLLECTIONS

A collection is a container to present knowledge assets together. It can serve the purpose of a folder, binder, file box, file drawer, rubber band, gem clip, or all of the above. It can gather the records for a person, a family, a place, a question, or a topic. It can organize the chapter, the lecture, or the presentation you are preparing.

You can gather things in multiple different ways and for multiple different purposes. Any item can appear in many different folders without taking up extra space. You can make your collection structure as small or as large as you need it to be—as simple or as complex.

QUICK TIP: Collections and parent items can be collapsed and expanded with your LEFT- and RIGHT-ARROW keys. If you select MY LIBRARY and click the LEFT ARROW, all subcollections will disappear beneath it. The RIGHT ARROW will expand it or any of its subcollections. The MINUS (-), clicked when MY LIBRARY is active, collapses all collections and subcollections. In the ITEM LIST, the PLUS (+) and MINUS keys collapse and expand all child items. If you want to close all child items in your entire list, select all (CTRL+A) and click the MINUS key.

CREATING COLLECTIONS

You have already created a collection with subcollections by importing your SAMPLE DATA. The import we did will rarely be your method. The collections in MY LIBRARY are created either by clicking the first icon on your Zotero toolbar, immediately below the FILE menu, or by right-clicking MY LIBRARY and choosing NEW COLLECTION. Then, type in your desired collection name and click OK.

To create a subcollection within an existing collection, right-click on the collection and choose NEW SUBCOLLECTION. Zotero places no limit on how many subcollections can be nested within each other. This ability to go deep with collections makes this a much more powerful organizational tool than many other research management tools.

NAMING COLLECTIONS TO CREATE ORDER AND EMPHASIS

You can change the name of a collection by double-clicking the collection name and typing new text or by right-clicking and choosing RENAME COLLECTION.

Zotero sorts its collections in alphanumeric order, in much the same way most of us organize a file drawer. If you have a set of folders you want to sort in a way other than alphabetically, use a numeral or letter at the start of the collection name. To change the order, change that character. If you have ten or more subcollections to put in order, put a zero in front of the single-digit numbers: 01, 02, 03, and so on.

FORCING A COLLECTION TO THE TOP

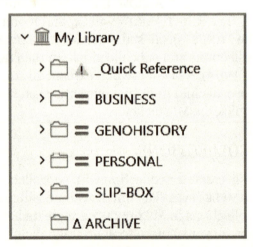

Emojis can force collections to the top or bottom, draw attention to major collections, or assign meaning to the text.

You can force a collection to the top or bottom of a set of same-level folders by using symbols or emojis that sort either before the letter "a" or after the letter "z." All numbers and most symbols and emoji characters fall before the letter "a" in alphanumeric sorting. If I want to force one collection to the top of a group, I tend to use an emoji that reflects the reason I'm driving it to the top. A caution flag is my favorite for putting things I most need to consult at the top.

ABOUT THE UNDERSCORE SYMBOL: Before discovering emojis, I simply typed an underscore before a label to move things to the top. This still works very well in collections. For the sort order of the ITEM LIST, however, the underscore no longer sorts to the top.

FORCING A COLLECTION TO THE BOTTOM

There may be subcollections you want to sort to the bottom of a set. Perhaps they contain things you rarely use, or information considered an appendix. While most emojis sort before "a" in alphanumeric order, some Greek letters sort after "z," like Ω (Omega), Ξ (Xi), and, my favorite, Δ (Delta).

EMPHASIZING A COLLECTION

Some Zotero users have only a few collections and do most of their organizing with tags. Others, like me, tend to create many folders and folders within folders. With the collections expanded, the navigation can become a visual challenge. Emojis or other symbols can help you to bring the primary folders into focus.

EMOJIS AND SYMBOLS

Emojis or symbol characters can be used wherever they are useful in your Zotero system—collections, notes, and tags. There are different methods of acquiring emojis, depending on your system. For Windows 11 users, you can quickly pull up a window of emoji options by holding down your Windows key (two keys to the left of your spacebar) and pressing your period (.) key. You can then browse or search for the sort of symbol that will serve you. Also, when you have used an emoji, you can paste it into Zotero's search window, and it will find all places you have used it.

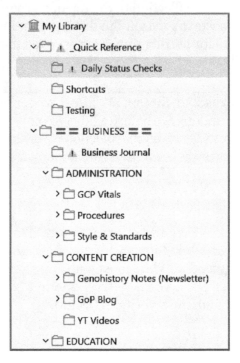

The bold equal sign emojis encasing the major collection called "BUSINESS" visually set it apart from the many other subcollections.

In the next exercise, you will create a legend in your Zotero database to keep up with the emojis you have used and what they signify for you. It will be the easiest way to get to the same emoji again for subsequent use. I keep my legend in a collection called QUICK REFERENCE, which is forced to the top of my library using an ALERT emoji.

EXERCISE 7. MANAGING COLLECTIONS

PREREQUISITE EXERCISE: 3

This exercise puts into practice the concepts described in this chapter, prepares your sample data to be a sandbox for future use, and creates a legend to hold emoji symbol definitions. For non-PC users, search to find how your computer accesses emojis and symbol characters and substitute your instructions for those in Step 5 below.

It is helpful to create a readily accessible note in your Zotero database containing any emojis or symbols you have chosen to use in your database. It aids in copying them for reuse and reminds you of the meaning you attached to them upon the original use.

When you are done with this book and working on your own research, you might want to experiment with things before you put them into practice in your research. So, this exercise renames your sample data to be your sandbox for experimentation.

STEP 1

Right-click on the QUICK GUIDE TO ZOTERO 7 collection. Select RE-NAME COLLECTION, type MY SANDBOX, and click OK.

STEP 2

To create a collection to hold items you will frequently consult, right-click on MY LIBRARY, choose NEW COLLECTION, type in QUICK REFERENCE, and click OK.

STEP 3

TO CREATE A LEGEND OF YOUR SYMBOLS AND EMOJIS, CLICK ON YOUR NEW QUICK REFERENCE COLLECTION. THEN CLICK THE NEW NOTE ICON ON YOUR DESKTOP TOOLBAR. SELECT NEW STANDALONE NOTE.

STEP 4

Click into the blank note field in your ITEM DETAILS pane. Type "Emoji and Symbols Legend," select HEADING 1 from the AA tool above the note, then press the ENTER key to go to a new line.

STEP 5

Hold down your WINDOWS key on your keyboard (with the Windows logo) and press your period key. In the emoji window that appears, type "alert." Click on the yellow triangle with the black exclamation mark (⚠), or your computer's equivalent. Type one or two spaces and "Quick access information" and press ENTER.

STEP 6

You will want your QUICK REFERENCE collection near the top of the COLLECTIONS pane, so you do not have to hunt for it in the growing mass of nested folders. Right now, it is at the bottom. The alert emoji should remain in your clipboard. Right-click on the QUICK REFERENCE collection and choose RENAME COLLECTION. Move your cursor in front of the title that is already there and paste the alert emoji. Type a space, then click OK. The collection should now be at the top, just below MY LIBRARY.

STEP 7

Your MY SANDBOX collection happens to be the last set of folders in your collection at present, but it will not be when you start adding your research. It will not be an active folder for you, so let's set it up to move to the bottom of your COLLECTION pane when new folders are added. We will be using a Greek symbol, rather than an emoji. Find your system's CHARACTER MAP app. For Windows users, click on the magnifying glass icon at the bottom of your Windows screen and start typing "Character Map." In the SEARCH FOR: field at the bottom of the app window, type "delta" and click ENTER. A set of characters will be displayed in the grid window. Click on the triangle—the Greek letter DELTA (Δ)—and click the SELECT button beneath the grid. Then click the COPY button and close the window. Right-click on MY SANDBOX, choose RENAME COLLECTION, move your cursor in front of the folder name, paste the DELTA symbol, then type a space, and click OK.

STEP 8

Now go back and click on the QUICK REFERENCE collection. Click on your legend in the ITEM LIST, then click into the note field. Add the Delta symbol to it, labeling it "Archived material."

Your workspace will now look something like this:

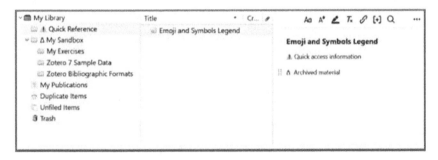

The newly named MY SANDBOX will always be near the bottom as an archived tool for future experimentation when needed. The QUICK REFERENCE collection will remain near the top, where you can quickly access your legend of emojis and symbols and store other things you regularly consult.

VIEWING SUBCOLLECTION CONTENTS

As you organize the material you are gathering in a collection, materials will be put out of sight into your subcollections. There will be times, though, when you want to view everything together—all the items that exist in a collection and its subcollections. When viewing the top-level collection, you can select SHOW ITEMS FROM SUBCOLLECTIONS from your VIEW menu. Every item will appear in the ITEM LIST.

QUICK PRACTICE: Click on the MY SANDBOX collection in your workspace. If the ITEM LIST has no contents, the SHOW ITEMS FROM SUBCOLLECTIONS feature is toggled off. Select VIEW from your workspace menu and toggle the feature on. Your ITEM LIST should now be filled with data.

ITEMS INSIDE COLLECTION FOLDERS

Despite appearances, every Zotero item exists in only one place: MY LIBRARY. As you add the items to collections, the items look and behave as though they reside inside the collection. But the items you see inside these folders are virtual links to the main item in MY LIBRARY. They are not copies. Any changes you make to an item in a collection folder change the main record in MY LIBRARY.

EXERCISE 8. TESTING THE VIRTUAL LINKS TO MY LIBRARY

PREREQUISITE EXERCISE: 3, 7

This exercise illustrates the idea of the "virtual link" that allows an item to appear in multiple collections when it only exists once in the database.

STEP 1

Click on MY LIBRARY in your COLLECTIONS pane. All your items will appear in the ITEM LIST. If they are not in alphabetical order, click on the TITLE label at the top to sort them. Find and click on the item labeled THE BEYOND KIN PROJECT. Notice that the AB-STRACT field is empty.

Step 2

In your Collections pane, click on Zotero 7 Sample Data. Now click on the item labeled The Beyond Kin Project. It appears to be a duplicate of the one you saw in My Library.

Step 3

In the Abstract field, type your own name.

Step 4

Click on My Library again, and then click its The Beyond Kin Project item. The Abstract field should now have your name in it. (Delete your name while you're there.)

As you can see, the collections appear to have duplicated these items. However, only one record exists—the one in My Library. The seeming duplicate in your sample data is a virtual link to the original record. If you change it here, you are changing the main record.

This allows you to find a desired item in multiple folders, though it exists only once. As you add notes, correct errors, or otherwise improve the record, your changes will appear wherever the record is used.

Quick Tip: To see all the collections containing an item, click the item in your Item List and hold down your Ctrl key. Zotero will highlight in yellow all applicable collections. If the item is in multiple subcollections, the highlighting will remain until you press Ctrl again.

EXERCISE 9. ADD A RECORD TO ANOTHER FOLDER

Prerequisite Exercises: 3, 7

In this exercise, we will look at more of the dynamics of collections.

STEP 1

Click on your ZOTERO 7 SAMPLE DATA folder. In the ITEM LIST, locate A HISTORY OF SUMTER COUNTY, ALABAMA, THROUGH 1886 and
drag it into your MY EXERCISES folder. Do you see that the item is
still in the SAMPLE DATA folder?

STEP 2

Click on the MY EXERCISES folder. Do you see a copy of the Sumter
County record there? Zotero always copies rather than moves a
link when you drag and drop items into different folders.

STEP 3

Let's say you meant to move the item, not to duplicate it. Go back
to the ZOTERO 7 SAMPLE DATA folder. Right-click the SUMTER
COUNTY record there and choose to REMOVE ITEM FROM COLLEC-
TION. It should now be gone from SAMPLE DATA and still present in
MY EXERCISES.
* * *

Remember that the two seeming copies of this item are just links
to one record. If you had chosen, instead, to REMOVE ITEM TO
TRASH, you would have removed the item from all locations, including MY LIBRARY. (It would remain in Zotero's TRASH until the
bin was emptied.)

From this point forward in the text, for simplicity's sake, I will
refer to adding and moving items without clarifying that it is operating on a link and not the real item in your collections. However,
moving and adding collections is not a virtual link, like it is for
items. In COLLECTIONS, add means add, and move means move,
which I will discuss in the next section.

QUICK TIP: If you want to drag an item from one collection to another and delete it from the original at the same time, there is a
keyboard shortcut. Drag the item to hover above the new collection. Hold down your SHIFT and CTRL keys simultaneously and
drop the item.

MOVING SUBCOLLECTIONS

The subcollections within a collection will organize themselves in alphanumeric order, as discussed. But you can move the folder into or out of another folder easily.
Drag the folder until it is on top of and highlights the desired folder. Drop it into the new location. Unlike items, it moves the folder rather than copying.

DELETING COLLECTIONS

If you want to remove a collection from Zotero, you may do it in one of two ways. Right-click the folder and choose one of the following options:

DELETE COLLECTION

If you choose this option, Zotero will delete the collection folder and any subcollection folders within it. But the items you had in the collection folders will continue to exist in MY LIBRARY and in any collections where you have put them. The folders will not be available from Zotero's TRASH.

DELETE COLLECTION AND ITEMS

This option will delete the selected collection folder, all subcollection folders, and all items they contain. The folders may not be recovered from the TRASH, but the items can be recovered until the TRASH is emptied.

4. MANAGING ATTACHMENTS

Attachments take you beyond the convenience of having access to your notes and a mechanism to cite your sources. They allow you to have digital copies of (or links to) your sources and supporting materials. They allow your Zotero database to become your map to or holder for every document, e-book, spreadsheet, map, photograph, sound file, or *whatever* supports your research. Entire public domain books are often digitized. You can carry your knowledge assets with you.

As you write a book, article, dissertation, report, or lecture, many sources you need to review are a few keystrokes away. You can mark them up, add notes, tag them, and connect them to related sources. However, there are a few important things to understand about attachments before you begin to bring large numbers of them into your library.

BEFORE YOU START ATTACHING

You will want to make your choices about attachments with long-term storage and access in mind. These choices determine if Zotero's free storage can give you what you need, or if you should spend a little to save time and effort. They determine whether you can capture web snapshots, access attachments when away from your computer, or easily access your attachments without Zotero.

As you attach files to items in your Zotero library, bring them in as standalone items, drag them in from your file manager, or import them with the ZOTERO CONNECTOR, the essential decision will be about where the attachments will be stored. Will you store them in your Zotero library, or will you link to them in an external location? While you are most likely to favor one option over the other, you can also take a hybrid approach, storing some items and linking to others.

There is no universally best arrangement. There is only the *best arrangement for you.*

Stored Versus Linked Attachments

Before we talk about how to use attachments, it's important to understand how your choices will impact Zotero's operation. In your normal daily work on your own computer, a stored attachment—embedded with your other Zotero data—will look and behave very much like one you have linked to in external storage (like Dropbox, Google Drive, or your computer's file manager). However, away from your computer the differences are more significant.

There are benefits and disadvantages to linked and stored arrangements (or a hybrid of the two, as I have), so it is best to know how each will work with your situation before you have gone too far down one path or another.

First, you should know that Zotero's development team strongly encourages the use of stored attachments, rather than linked. Its documentation describes it aptly as the "more seamless" method. The team can support what is in your Zotero database, not the software or data outside of it to which you have linked. Also, the reasonable amount paid for Zotero Storage (which you will need if you store your attachments in your Zotero database) funds the Zotero operation, benefiting us all. (See Zotero Storage[1] for current pricing.)

You may already know exactly what you want to do. If so, wonderful. You are all set. If you are not sure, take some time to digest the section in Chapter 9 called Stored or Linked Attachments > In-depth Considerations.

While you are mulling it over, start with the free plan and experiment with both linked and stored attachments, keeping under your 300-MB free storage limit. Give yourself enough time with the product to know what is best for you and your projects.

CREATING FILE ATTACHMENTS

In Zotero, attachments can stand alone, added directly to a collection. Or they can be attached as a child to a reference item. They cannot be attached to a note or another attachment. An attachment is created by one of the following means:

---

[1] https://www.zotero.org/storage

DRAG-AND-DROP ATTACHMENTS

To conveniently create an attachment from a file that currently sits on your hard drive, drag and drop it from your file manager. If you drop it on the parent reference item or into the ITEM LIST or a folder, it will become a stored item. To link to the attachment, instead, hold down your CTRL and SHIFT keys as you drop it on the parent item or folder. You can drag and drop a batch of attachments at the same time, which becomes very helpful when moving existing files into Zotero.

IMPORTED ATTACHMENTS

If you are fortunate, many of your items, including attachments, will be created by automated tools like ZOTERO CONNECTOR or by an import from other reference software. Your settings will determine what sort of automation you are willing to allow. Visit EDIT > SETTINGS > GENERAL in the FILE HANDLING section to see your options. You may choose to have Zotero automatically capturing PDFs, web snapshots, and/or EPUB files during ZOTERO CONNECTOR imports, a great convenience. Be aware, though, that any item captured into your database will count against your ZOTERO STORAGE limits. These attachments can use up your free 300 MB storage allotment very quickly, so if you plan to have Zotero capturing these items, you should get paid storage.

ATTACHMENT BY ZOTERO'S MENU

To add an attachment through Zotero's menu, select the desired folder, right-click on the item in your ITEM LIST and choose ADD ATTACHMENT. Choose one of the following three options:

FILE

A file attached this way becomes a part of Zotero's data. If you are syncing your files to Zotero's online cloud storage, your attachments will be synced, along with your source reference, and available wherever you have internet access. Stored attachments count toward your ZOTERO STORAGE allotment if synced. See STORED OR

LINKED ATTACHMENTS—IN-DEPTH CONSIDERATIONS in Chapter 9 for more information.

LINKED FILE

This option links Zotero to an attachment stored on your computer or another external location. It makes the file quickly accessible from Zotero but keeps it separate from Zotero's main data storage. It will not be synced to Zotero's cloud. You can link to documents that are synced to external cloud storage, so long as they have a physical copy on your device. See STORED OR LINKED ATTACHMENTS—IN-DEPTH CONSIDERATIONS in Chapter 9 for more information. If you link to a searchable PDF or text file, Zotero will include the text of your attachment in its searches. If you log into Zotero on a remote computer—away from your hard drive—you will not be able to access the linked attachments through Zotero. If you have stored them in external cloud storage, however, you can access them separately through that cloud's website.

WEB LINK

This option links an item or creates a freestanding link to a web-based resource. This option opens a small window, asking for the LINK and TITLE of your URL.

You already have a URL field in your source reference record, which will serve you perfectly well in most cases. But this link allows you to identify multiple resources online that support your research and to link Google Sheets, Google Docs, and other online sources that have no copy on your hard drive.

In the case of web links, Zotero will only search what you have typed into the title. It will not search the contents of the resource to which you are linking. Therefore, you might want to add a few defining terms in the title that will help you to find your way back to this resource in a Zotero search.

———

The first two attachment options are created in virtually the same way, by browsing to find the desired attachment on your hard drive or other device. And from your perspective, they will look and operate almost identically in Zotero if you are at your own computer. You can only tell them apart visually by the icon Zotero uses. If you choose the LINKED FILE option, the file's icon appears in the ITEM LIST as a document with chain links. If you choose FILE, the icon is a document without the chain link.

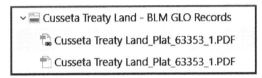

Two identical copies of the same PDF are attached to an item in the ITEM LIST. The chain link on the first one tells you it is a linked attachment. The second is stored in the Zotero database.

EXERCISE 10. ATTACH A LINKED PDF

PREREQUISITE EXERCISES: 3, 7

To test Zotero's ability to attach documents and to prepare for later exercises, this exercise will pull a PDF from the web to attach to an item in your ZOTERO 7 SAMPLE DATA folder.

STEP 1

In your web browser, go to this URL: https://genohistory.com/PDFsample.pdf. (This is case-sensitive, and do not type the final period.)

STEP 2

A toolbar on the PDF should offer a button to save or download the PDF to your computer. A copy will be deposited into your computer's DOWNLOADS folder. For simplicity's sake, we will leave the PDF there, though you would normally save it to another location for long-term safekeeping.

STEP 3

In Zotero, select the ZOTERO 7 SAMPLE DATA folder in the COLLECTIONS pane and find an existing item labeled DESCRIPTIVE PAMPHLET OF HILLSBOROUGH COUNTY, FLORIDA.

STEP 4

Right-click on the pamphlet item and click ADD ATTACHMENT >
LINKED FILE. Browse to your computer's DOWNLOADS folder and
select the PDFSAMPLE.PDF you saved in STEP 3. Click OPEN. It will
now appear as a child item beneath the Hillsborough pamphlet
item in your ITEM LIST. Its icon should display a chain link.

STEP 5

Click on the parent item again, view the ITEM DETAILS, and scroll
down to the ATTACHMENTS section. If it is not expanded, click on
the section title to expand it. You should see a PREVIEW PANE containing the new attachment. Click on the arrows at the bottom of
the preview to see how you can move through the pages of the attachment without opening it. The PREVIEW PANE works for PDF,
EPUB, HTML, and image files.

RENAMING ATTACHMENTS

As you collect materials from a variety of sources, the names vary
in format. Some attachment names will describe the contents, and
some will be a string of coded text and numbers—making sense
only to the institution that created them.

You can leave the names as they are if you prefer. Or you may
change the names to bring consistency. There are several ways to
go about it, and things to consider as you do.

FILE RENAMING SETTINGS

The FILE RENAMING section sets your preferences for naming PDF,
e-book, image, audio, and video attachments as you bring them
into your Zotero database. If you prefer to keep the original names
or to rename things manually, deselect AUTOMATICALLY RENAME
LOCALLY ADDED FILES.

If you want Zotero to rename new attachments according to an
established pattern, mark AUTOMATICALLY RENAME LOCALLY ADDED
FILES. If you want the original filename to remain on the file you
are linking to outside Zotero, deselect RENAME LINKED FILES.

> **File Renaming**
>
> Zotero automatically renames downloaded files based on the details of the parent item (title, author, etc.). You can choose to rename files added from your computer as well.
>
> ☑ Automatically rename locally added files
>
>   Rename files of these types:
>
>   ☑ PDF   ☑ Ebook   ☐ Image   ☐ Audio   ☐ Video
>
>   ☑ Rename linked files
>
>   Customize Filename Format...

In EDIT > SETTINGS > GENERAL, the FILE RENAMING section determines if and how new attachments will be renamed.

If automatically renaming your attachments, Zotero puts an internal label, "PDF" for PDF documents, for example. The file's name in your computer's file manager defaults to a string that draws information from the parent item's metadata. By default, it strings together the creator's last name, creation year, and title truncated at 100 characters. You can alter this arrangement by clicking CUSTOMIZE FILENAME FORMAT. The documentation offers multiple ways to control the output, using simple coding.

MANUALLY ALTER ATTACHMENT FILENAME

If your settings do not alter the filename automatically when you first attach a file, the file will have the name its original creator gave it. When you click on the attachment in your ITEM LIST, the ITEM DETAILS will display an attachment title at the top and the actual stored filename at the bottom. You can click in either or both fields and rename them.

LET ZOTERO ALTER INDIVIDUAL ATTACHMENT NAME

If you want Zotero to alter a child attachment's filename using the parent data and the template in your settings, right-click on the item in the ITEM LIST and choose RENAME FILE FROM PARENT'S METADATA. You cannot undo the change, except manually.

PARENTLESS FILES

You can bring a file into Zotero without a parent record, either by doing ADD ATTACHMENT > FILE or by dragging a file from your file manager and dropping it in the ITEM LIST. However, in most cases, you will want a parent item, documenting the file's source. To add a parent to an orphaned attachment, right-click on it and choose CREATE PARENT ITEM. If you have an identifying number like a DOI or if the attachment has its own identifying metadata, Zotero can fill in the source information. Otherwise, you can manually fill in the details.

SEARCHING THE CONTENTS OF ATTACHMENTS

Zotero can search the contents of four types of attachments: searchable PDFs, EPUBs, HTML snapshots, and plain-text files. In SETTINGS > ADVANCED > FULL-TEXT CACHE, you can set limits on how many characters of a document will be indexed to maximize search speed. See more about how to make PDFs searchable in Chapter 7.

SETTING A BASE DIRECTORY AND LINKED ATTACHMENT RELATIVE PATH

If you choose to link to your attachments externally, rather than storing them in Zotero, think carefully about where you store them and how you name them on your hard drive or external drive. As you browse and link to the attachments, you are essentially giving Zotero an address—a path—where it can find the item. If you later delete, rename, or move the attachment on your drive, Zotero's link will be broken.

You cannot guarantee, even if you are very careful, that you will always be able to keep your attachment files in the original location. Computers become obsolete or damaged. Operating systems are upgraded, forcing unexpected changes. Things simply change. You want to be able to easily move your attachment files from one place to another without breaking the links you have created to the original address.

If you are using Zotero on multiple computers, you may find that the address that works on one computer cannot be matched exactly on the other. You will want to be able to use Zotero seamlessly on each computer.

Zotero offers a way to handle major file movements and the multiple-computer situation by allowing you to designate a BASE DIRECTORY, with all your files organized inside it. You set your base directory in SETTINGS > ADVANCED > FILES AND FOLDERS. If for any reason you want to move all your files to a new location—a new computer, an external hard drive, a cloud location—you can move them all intact to a new base directory and tell Zotero what the new location is.

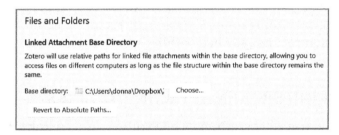

Organize linked attachments in whatever way you wish—so long as they remain at the same path relative to your BASE DIRECTORY.

As you see in the image above, my base directory is

C:\USERS\DONNA BAKER\DROPBOX\ZOTERO ATTACHMENTS

Within this base directory, I have created subdirectories in my Dropbox cloud to hold all my business and personal files. Inside my GENOHISTORY folder, for example I organize everything geno-history-related as I want it.

C:\USERS\DONNA BAKER\DROPBOX\ZOTERO ATTACHMENTS\GENO-HISTORY

My base directory can change, but everything in GENOHISTORY must keep its same order and filenames to preserve the links. This

creates a "relative path" for Zotero. Each of my linked attachments
is always in the same place, relative to the base directory.

Let's say I have decided to move all my attachments to an external hard drive assigned the drive letter D by my computer. The external drive doesn't have the Users folder like a PC would. Zotero
is still looking for all the attachments at the old location, and I
could break hundreds or thousands of links by moving the files,
without designating a changed base directory. To prevent that
breakage, I assign a new base directory of:
D:\DROPBOX\ZOTERO ATTACHMENTS

I then move the GENOHISTORY folder from the old location into
my new ZOTERO ATTACHMENTS on the new computer. When I click
on an attachment link in Zotero, it knows to look on the D drive.
Assuming everything in the GENOHISTORY folder remains in the
same structure it already had within the new BASE DIRECTORY,
Zotero will find it.

RESTORING BROKEN ATTACHMENT LINKS

Inevitably, you will occasionally encounter a broken link to an attachment. While the relative path just described can eliminate major breakage, you will occasionally move or rename a file,
accidentally or on purpose.

If a link has been broken, you will know it when you attempt to
open the attachment and see this message:

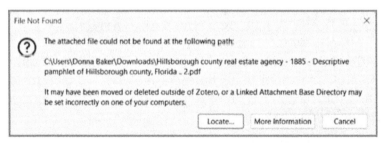

Click LOCATE to search for the missing attachment.
Zotero will restore the link when you have located the
file.

You can handle it in one of three ways:

- Browse to find a misplaced attachment using the Locate button.

- Replace the file in the designated location.

- Delete the attachment link if the file no longer exists.

5. ZOTERO CONNECTORS FOR IN-STANT DATA ENTRY

The ZOTERO CONNECTOR feature first hooked me on the Zotero product, making it unbeatable among my options. This browser extension allows you to capture bibliographic data from a web page, entering it into Zotero with the push of a button. With thousands of bibliographic citations to enter while working on my dissertation, this saved me hundreds of hours and much aggravation. Even better, it did a more thorough and much more accurate job of the data entry than I would have done by manual typing.

The ZOTERO CONNECTOR adds a new icon to your browser window for capturing bibliographic information to Zotero. The icon image changes, based on the nature of the information being presented.

INSTALLING ZOTERO CONNECTOR

If you followed my instructions in Chapter 1, the connector is probably already on your computer. If not, you can do it now. Zotero offers connectors for Chrome, Firefox, Edge, and Safari web browsers. The ZOTERO CONNECTORS can all be downloaded from the Zotero website by choosing INSTALL BROWSER CONNECTOR from your TOOLS menu.

I use the Chrome browser, as do most of you, so the instructions here will be for Chrome. For Chrome, select INSTALL. For all other browsers, select SHOW ALL CONNECTORS and follow Zotero's instructions for your browser. Chrome will present a notification about adding the extension to the browser environment. Choose ADD EXTENSION.

Your Chrome browser will give you a second notice that the extension has been added, and a tiny icon will now appear at the top line of your browser window, just to the right of your URL field. The icon will change shapes, depending on what type of information Zotero perceives to be displayed on the screen. If you are on an informational website, it will look like a computer screen. If you are looking at a book advertisement on Amazon, it will look like a book. Let your cursor rest on top of it. If you see the tooltip SAVE TO ZOTERO, you have located the proper icon.

This icon will become your method to populate your Zotero research items with citation information someone typed. You will love the work it saves.

OTHER METHODS TO CAPTURE DATA

If you have none of the supported browsers or are working on a device that does not have Zotero installed, you can simulate the connector function by pasting a URL to the search field on this webpage: SAVE TO ZOTERO PAGE.[1] Bookmark it on your device, so you can get there easily when you have a site to save to Zotero. The ZOTERO CONNECTOR will send the data to your WEB LIBRARY at ZOTERO.ORG, and then sync it to your desktop the next time you open it.

USING THE ZOTERO CONNECTOR

Your Zotero desktop software must be open for ZOTERO CONNECTOR to send bibliographic data directly to it. You can use ZOTERO CONNECTOR on any browser for which you enabled the plugin.

I find it most valuable and accurate to capture items from library and archive catalogs online if they have made their metadata visible to the web. The megacatalog called WORLDCAT[2] is enabled for Zotero and is one of the best places you can gather bibliographic data. Zotero also captures book data from Amazon. If it does not recognize bibliographic data within the displayed website, ZOTERO CONNECTOR assumes that you want to capture this as

---

[1] https://www.zotero.org/save
[2] https://worldcat.org/

a webpage, and it draws the proper bibliographic information for that.

If a library or website does not appear to work properly with Zotero—capturing everything as a website—consider asking the information provider to make their metadata accessible. Instructions can be found on Zotero's website in a topic called EXPOSING YOUR METADATA.[3]

ZOTERO CONNECTOR will extract the information and create a new Zotero record. The record will always be displayed in MY LIBRARY, but it will also appear in the Zotero subcollection active at the time the connector button is used.

EXERCISE 11. CREATE A ZOTERO RECORD WITH ZOTERO CONNECTOR

Let's say you want a book that WorldCat tells you is in your local library. You can add it to Zotero ahead of your visit. It will be primed and ready for that day when you go to the library, get the book, and take notes. Do the following:

STEP 1

In Zotero, click on your MY EXERCISES collection.

STEP 2

In your web browser, open WORLDCAT to the *Early Settlers of Pickens County*[4] book by James Dolphus Johnson Jr. (If by chance this record is no longer in the catalog by the time of this printing, pick another book.)

STEP 3

With the book record displayed on the screen, click on the ZOTERO CONNECTOR icon in the top right corner, which will most likely appear as a blue book. Zotero will present a small window, telling you where it intends to save this record. It will pause for a few

---

[3] https://www.zotero.org/support/dev/exposing_metadata
[4] https://worldcat.org/title/27420709

seconds to give you a chance to change its destination by clicking
on the drop-down arrow button.

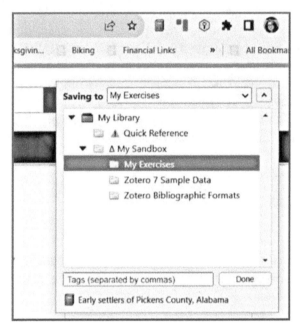

*ZOTERO CONNECTOR gives you a few seconds to decide if
you want to save the new asset to someplace other than
the currently open collection in Zotero.*

If you do not click the dropdown list within that time, it assumes you wish to put the item into the folder already open in
Zotero. For our purposes, do not change the location it will be
saved to.

The new record should be in your MY EXERCISES collection,
having pulled the record from the WORLDCAT database.

Thanks to the wonders of "metadata," Zotero knew exactly what
information to put in each field. You will always want to check behind this process because Zotero might not always have it right. Or
the person who cataloged the information in the library catalog
might have been inaccurate or incomplete.

This tool can be especially helpful in populating Zotero with existing research, starting with your own personal library. You can

enter your books by their ISBNs or find the books in an online catalog and let the catalog do a lot of your work for you.

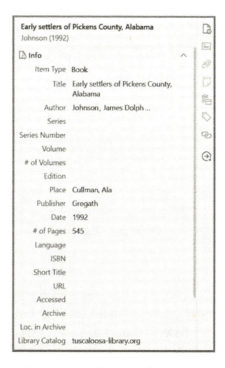

The ZOTERO CONNECTOR has saved you typing all of this, bringing it into your database with the click of a button.

PULLING MULTIPLE ITEMS WITH A SINGLE ZOTERO CONNECTOR ACTION

Depending on the setup of the website from which you are pulling data, you might have the option to select and pull multiple items into Zotero. Take, for example, the Google Scholar website. You can search on a topic and bring up a list of sources that might address that topic. The ZOTERO CONNECTOR icon presented is a folder, offering the first clue that you might be retrieving more than one item. Clicking on the folder brings up a list of possible items to import as citation items. You may select the ones you want, click OK, choose the Zotero folder you want to deposit them in, and click DONE.

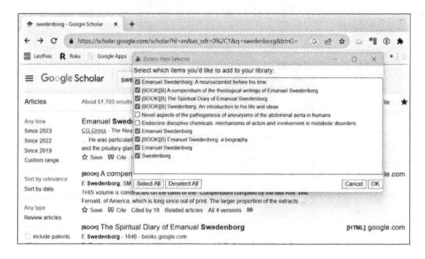

The elements selected in this window are imported as items into Zotero.

SUMMARY

Though the ZOTERO CONNECTOR is technically an ADD-ON, the browser connectors are developed and supported by Zotero. You should consider it an essential part of your Zotero toolkit. It will magnify your effectiveness at research and remove much of the tedium of data entry.

6. SORTING, SEARCHING, AND FILTERING YOUR RESEARCH

As knowledge assets grow from hundreds to thousands to potentially tens of thousands, finding them again is the key to successful research and analysis. Zotero creates multiple layers of findability, ensuring the best possible success in making your research count.

BASIC SORTING

Zotero allows you to sort a selected collection on any of the displayed fields in your ITEM LIST. If you have selected MY LIBRARY in your COLLECTIONS pane, you are sorting your entire collection. Sort the items by clicking on the heading of the ITEM LIST column that holds the values you want to sort. Clicking a column heading a second time will reverse the sort order. Fields with no values will be sorted to the back end of a sorted range in ascending order. In other words, they will be behind the largest number, the Z words, or the Greek symbols in the column.

When sorting the DATE field, Zotero will not sort the items in numerical or alphabetical order. It will arrange the material in proper date order, based on its understanding of your date format. Therefore, though your database might include a mixture of date formats—1/5/1854, 5 January 1854, Jan 5, 1854, and 1854-01-05 all being the same date—Zotero knows where they belong in the larger sorted collection.

CHOOSING AND CONTROLLING COLUMNS

You can choose the columns to display in your ITEM LIST from nearly all available fields. This allows you to sort and search with desired precision. The available fields can be found by right-clicking on any of the heading labels above the items.

The most-used fields are displayed at the top of the selection list, but many others are available in the MORE COLUMNS option. You are also able to choose a SECONDARY SORT field.

You may resize the columns by dragging the thin gray line between the column headings to the right or left. You can rearrange the columns by clicking and dragging the heading label, dropping it where you want the column to be. Select a field a second time to deselect it.

EXERCISE 12. ADD, ARRANGE, AND REMOVE COLUMN IN ITEM LIST

To practice these skills, this exercise will sort your ITEM LIST by their ITEM TYPE. You will make it your first column, sort by it, and then remove it. Click on your ZOTERO 7 SAMPLE DATA collection and follow these steps:

STEP 1

In your ITEM LIST, right-click one of the headings and select the ITEM TYPE from the displayed list. If you do not see it, click on MORE COLUMNS to display the rest of the fields, and select it from there.

STEP 2

The ITEM TYPE now shows in your list, probably not in the first position. Click and hold the ITEM TYPE label above the new column and drag it to the left until you drop it on the first header field—probably your TITLE. The ITEM TYPE should now be your first column.

Item Type	Title	▲	Date Added	Creator
Map	Survey of the Town of Alexandria		2/11/2021, 9:31:...	Lindsey
Journal Article	> Swedenborg		10/14/2023, 5:5...	Frethingham
Presentation	Talladega Incorporated		7/10/2021, 9:46:...	*Settlement
Web Page	Tax Assessment Report--McClell...		1/7/2021, 4:09:5...	Alabama--Cal...
Newspaper Article	> Taxes (Pickup Locations)		1/19/2023, 12:0...	
E-mail	> Taylor Family Data		12/4/2017, 9:59:...	Taylor Jr.

You may add, resize, and rearrange columns in the Zotero ITEM LIST. Here, the ITEM TYPE column has been dragged in front of the TITLE.

STEP 3

Click on the ITEM TYPE label to sort your items in ITEM TYPE order.

STEP 4

To remove the ITEM TYPE column, right-click again on the ITEM LIST heading row and choose ITEM TYPE, this time deselecting it.

ITEM SEARCHING

Zotero offers a search box above the ITEM LIST, which gives several options for filtering the search for items. You do not have to recall exact phrases. If you do not type in quotation marks around terms, Zotero will find any record that contains the terms you enter in the field, regardless of the order of the search terms or the fields in which those terms exist. If you use quotation marks, Zotero will shift into ADVANCED SEARCH mode and search for the exact phrase as it exists in the system—not considering capitalization.

You have these research options in the ITEM SEARCH:

TITLE, CREATOR, YEAR

Zotero will search only the three fields most populated in typical items: the TITLE, the CREATOR, and the YEAR of publication or creation.

ALL FIELDS & TAGS

Zotero will seek your search terms in any reference item field or in the tags you have assigned.

EVERYTHING

Zotero will search all reference fields, tags, notes, PDFs, EPUBs, HTML snapshots, and text files for your search terms.

ADVANCED SEARCHING

If the ITEM SEARCH operation brings you too many results, you can search with greater precision using Zotero's ADVANCED SEARCH.

ADVANCED SEARCHING

You can create multiple criteria, choosing to retrieve items that match any or all specified criteria. You may seek a specific word or phrase within a specific field. You can have Zotero choose items that do not have a specific word or phrase in a specific field. And you can save a search to use again, if helpful.

The search criteria can contain one or more elements—each further expanding or refining the set of items Zotero will retrieve or exclude. You add or remove criteria lines using the MINUS and PLUS icons at the end of a displayed line.

With each line, you will choose the field to search, the evaluation option, and the content you are evaluating in your search.

Zotero's ADVANCED SEARCH feature allows you to get very specific in the search for an elusive record.

SEARCH PARAMETERS

SEARCH IN LIBRARY

The SEARCH IN LIBRARY question defaults to MY LIBRARY and, in most cases, will remain that. If you have any GROUP LIBRARIES connected to your account, you may use them, as well. RSS FEEDS are treated as libraries for searching in this context, also.

MATCH

With the MATCH question, you alert Zotero to whether you want only the items that match all criteria you are about to enter, or whether you want every item that matches any of them.

FIELD EVALUATION CRITERIA

FIELD

The field element (defaults to TITLE) is chosen from a drop-down list of all available fields in your ITEM LIST, including collections, tags, and notes.

EVALUATION OPTION

The evaluation option (defaults to CONTAINS) determines what content will cause an item to be included or excluded in the search results. It is chosen from a drop-down list that changes, depending on the field you choose in the first element. If you are evaluating the NOTES field, for example, your options will be CONTAINS and DOES NOT CONTAIN. The CREATOR field includes both of those, but adds IS and IS NOT, so you can evaluate the entire contents of the field. DATE fields will allow you to evaluate before and after criteria, including whether the record contains a date within a certain number of days, months, or years before the current date.

CONTENT

In the content element, you might be presented with a drop-down list or a text box, depending upon the type of field you are searching. Here, you tell Zotero what information you want it to retrieve (or avoid) in the selected field, as it chooses the items to retrieve for your review.

Plus or Minus

The tiny PLUS and MINUS signs at the end of each criteria line let you either add another criteria line (PLUS) or delete the current one (MINUS). If you choose in the MATCH field to include items that match "any" of the criteria, adding lines will expand your search results. If you only want those that match "all" criteria, adding more evaluation criteria lines will shorten your search results.

Filtering Display Options

You may further refine what Zotero finds and how it displays what it finds by clicking on any of these options:

Search Subcollections

In most cases, you will be searching your entire data set, the MY LIBRARY collection, for which this option has no use. But if you choose a specific collection to search (by selecting COLLECTION as your field element on one of your criteria lines), this option will allow you to specify whether the subcollections within that collection will be included.

Show Only Top-Level Items

This option controls how Zotero will display the retrieved items. If this field is selected, Zotero will show only the items in which the reference record contains the specified content. It will not pull child items attached to the reference. If it is not selected, Zotero will display the entire set of items associated with the matching record—its parent or child items, if available, and any other items attached to its parent. Zotero will display the item that contains the matching record in full resolution. The other items will be grayed out, but visible.

INCLUDE PARENT AND CHILD ITEMS OF MATCHING ITEMS

If this is selected, Zotero treats the parent of a matching child record the same way it treats the child. Both will be displayed in full resolution. If you have selected this and selected the SHOW ONLY TOP-LEVEL ITEMS option, only the parent items will be displayed.

SEARCH OPTIONS

SEARCH

This option will run a search using the criteria you set. The results will appear in the display window at the bottom. You can sort the items using the labels above them— which work like the ITEM LIST labels. If you find the one you want, double-click on it, and it will close the search window and take you to the item in the ITEM LIST.

CLEAR

The CLEAR button will empty the evaluation criteria you entered. But it will leave the window open for you to repopulate the criteria and try again.

SAVE SEARCH

If you click the SAVE SEARCH button, Zotero will create an item in your COLLECTIONS pane, and allow you to give it a name. With this, you can repeat a search easily, showing the retrieved items in the main desktop view, rather than in the ADVANCED SEARCH popup window. Your saved searches will appear as a folder icon with a magnifying glass in the COLLECTIONS pane.

EXERCISE 13. DO AN ADVANCED SEARCH

Admittedly, we have so little data in Zotero at present that a complex search might seem a waste of time. But let's do it anyway, in preparation for the day that you have 8,000 items in your database—many entered years ago and no longer remembered well, if at all. Imagine you have collected hundreds of maps, books, articles, and images related to the history of Louisiana. You want to pinpoint an actual map you vaguely recall of Louisiana in the nineteenth century. Do the following:

STEP 1

Click on the ADVANCED SEARCH icon on the toolbar to bring up the ADVANCED SEARCH criteria window.

STEP 2

Leave the top two items as they default. In the first line of search criteria, enter TITLE as the field, CONTAINS as the criteria, and LOUISIANA as the content. Click the plus button at the end of the line. You should see a list of items in the results window.

STEP 3

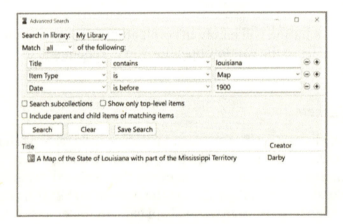

As each line of criteria is added, the results in the window shrink.

Enter the next two criteria lines as you see in the image above. The results should shrink to one.

STEP 4

To make this search available again later, click the SAVE SEARCH
button. Enter a meaningful label like 19TH-CENTURY LA MAPS and
click OK. You will now have an item toward the bottom of the MY
LIBRARY portion of your COLLECTIONS pane. Click on it at any time
to bring your search up in your ITEM LIST.

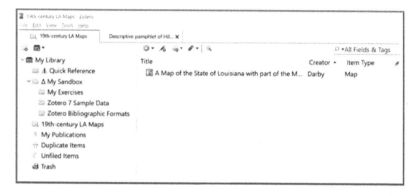

*If you expect to repeat a search set often, the SAVE
SEARCH feature will create a link in the COLLECTIONS
pane that repeats the search.*

SAVED SEARCH USES

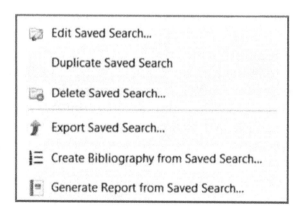

*Right-click on a SAVED SEARCH to bring up a list of
options for things you can do with the results.*

Once you create a SAVED SEARCH, there are several things you can do with it. You can edit the criteria, duplicate it, or delete it. You can export the results, create a bibliography, or create a report. You get to these options by right-clicking on the SAVED SEARCH line in your COLLECTIONS pane and choosing one of the displayed options.

COLLECTIONS SEARCHING

Collections are searched separately from Zotero items. Above the COLLECTIONS pane, a magnifying glass icon opens the FILTER COLLECTIONS field. Zotero will filter your COLLECTIONS pane view based on any string you type in this field. Rather than simply displaying the name of the matching collection, however, it will display the nested collections that hold it. This allows you to recall not just that the collection exists, but where you stored it. To restore the full view of collections, click the X in the FILTER COLLECTIONS field.

NOTES SEARCHING

Notes can be searched individually or as a part of the entire collection. When you are in a note in either the ITEM DETAILS or the right pane of the ZOTERO READER, you can click the magnifying glass icon on the pane's toolbar to search. This also allows you to search and replace text by marking the REPLACE field on the search bar.

Notes are included in the ITEM SEARCH, but you can search *only* notes from within the ZOTERO READER. A PDF, EPUB, or HTML file must be open for the READER to be accessible. Any notes attached to the open file will appear at the top under ITEM NOTES. Beneath those, under ALL NOTES, all other notes will appear. The SEARCH field is accessed at the top of the pane by clicking the magnifying glass icon.

You can also use the ADVANCED SEARCH feature to narrow a search exclusively to notes.

OPEN TAB SEARCHING

A down arrow (v) to the left of the sync icon on the tab bar allows you to search the open READER tabs by a string of text in the title. This is helpful when you have many READER sessions open and need to quickly find one. You can click on the item and bring it to the front, drag and drop tabs into a new order, or close a document from this window.

FILTERING WITH TAGS

You can bring up all the items with the same assigned tag by using the TAG SELECTOR pane in the bottom left corner of your desktop workspace. By default, Zotero displays all available tags. To reduce the options to a subset of all the tags, type a few letters of the tag title in the search box at the bottom of the window.

The dotted icon to the right of the search box allows you to restore the full set of tags if you have isolated them to a filtered selection. It also allows you to hide AUTOMATIC TAGS, those created when items are imported with ZOTERO CONNECTOR. You may also delete these automatic tags.

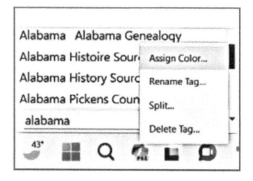

You can filter available tags by entering keywords in the search box. If you right-click on a tag, you have options to color-code, rename, split terms in, and delete a tag.

7. THE ZOTERO READER: PDFS, EPUBS, AND HTML SNAPSHOTS

Zotero 7 includes built-in technology for reading, marking up, and annotating PDF, EPUB, and HTML documents. The markups and annotations can be written into item notes, as well, which saves time in documenting your research. ZOTERO READER is an expanded version of what was simply the PDF READER in Zotero 6. Because its features will be so new to many long-time Zotero users, I will go more in-depth on it than I normally might in a Quick Guide. Many researchers will spend most of their Zotero time here.

If you prefer to use external software products to read and annotate your PDF, EPUB, and HTML files, you can do that. You right-click on the file in your ITEM LIST and select SHOW FILE. This will open your system's file manager to the folder that holds the item. You can then open it in whatever software tool you prefer.

ZOTERO READER WORKSPACE

The ZOTERO READER workspace is multilayered, with a robust set of tools and functions. Supporting plugins—especially one called BETTER NOTES—make it even more powerful and will be described in future Quick Guides. The various functions use three panes, with the middle one dedicated to the document and always in view. The left and right panes can be resized, changed in function, or hidden.

The left pane can display all the annotations you have created for the displayed document. When more than one color has been applied to annotations, a box appears at the bottom of this pane, allowing you to filter to notes with a particular color. For PDFs, it can display all page thumbnails. And for all document formats, it can display the table of contents or document outline, if the document has proper heading styles applied.

The right pane can display the reference information for the document or its parent item. While in that pane, it can show the tags or related items. Alternatively, it can show a list of all available notes, displaying any connected to the active item at the top.

When you click on a note, it will open and can be edited and tagged.

The middle pane can be marked up and annotated. One of its best features is the ability to send an underlined or highlighted patch of text to a note connected to this item. The text's source is cited and links back to the main document. This allows you to immediately jump from the note to the spot where it is marked in a document.

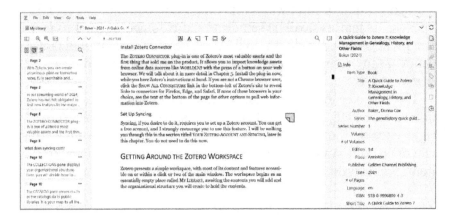

For most, Zotero's very robust Reader technology eliminates the need to view PDF, EPUB, and HTML documents in external software.

The features are slightly different between the three formats. I will describe them here, but we can expect that new features will be added regularly in the future.

PDF (Portable Document Format) Features

PDFs have long been a popular format in portable documents. PDFs may be attached to an item in your Item List manually. Or, depending on a website's permissions and your Zotero Settings, Zotero may import PDFs along with citation data through Zotero Connector. To set Zotero for the import of PDFs with citations, check Automatically attach associated PDFs and other files when saving items on the General tab of your Settings, in the File Handling section. When activated, any use of Zotero

CONNECTOR may import a PDF or other file, with no effort on your part. This is tremendously helpful in gathering research but will also rapidly fill free Zotero storage. Without paid storage, do not activate this feature.

Zotero has built in the most essential features of PDF readers, eliminating the need to have separate software or to port documents in and out of Zotero. For those who use high-end features of a product like Adobe DC, there might still be a need for external software, particularly for things like signature routing.

Your annotations and markups in Zotero exist in an independent layer that sits above the original PDF document. The original PDF remains intact beneath the markup layer. Therefore, if you open a PDF you have marked up in Zotero outside of the product, your Zotero annotations will not appear. You can export a copy of the PDF with markings, however, if you want them visible in other software programs.

The practice of keeping the original PDF separate from the annotation layer offers important efficiency in syncing. Some of your PDFs might be 500 pages long. If your annotations were being saved into the original PDF, every change you make would force a full sync of your 500-page document and its annotations. By putting the additions into independent layers, the syncing will only pick up what has changed, leaving the large bulk of the document untouched.

The READER'S toolset for marking up PDFs offers highlighting, underlining, text boxes, and drawing in multiple colors—a limited color palette that is expected to expand in future versions. Highlighting and underlining require the PDF to be editable, having an underlying text layer, rather than being simply a snapshot. The READER also has sticky notes and an image capture tool, which lets you grab a picture of a piece of the PDF. This is especially useful if the PDF has images or tables embedded. Each annotation can be commented upon and tagged, lending a remarkable potency to research—especially to collaborative research.

These features work both on PDFs stored in Zotero and those linked externally.

Optical Character Recognition (OCR)

Zotero can search for a particular string of text in attached PDF files that have a searchable text layer. It is important to distinguish a searchable PDF from one that merely looks like it should be. As mentioned above, some PDFs are just a snapshot of text. Your eyes can process the letters as words, but a computer simply sees ink on paper unless an invisible text layer hides behind the image of the page. There is a quick way to tell if your document is readable as text. Click on a word on the PDF page. If the PDF puts a cursor into the word or selects the word, your PDF should be searchable. If instead, the entire page is highlighted or nothing is highlighted, the page most likely is not searchable.

Some PDF software can convert the images of words into real text by a process called Optical Character Recognition, or OCR. While not always perfect in its translation, even a bad OCR scan can sometimes be helpful in making your document or the text within it findable. There has been a plugin called Zotero-OCR that was able to run this utility on PDFs, but as of this writing, it has not been updated for Zotero 7. There are some internet tools that offer free OCR services until another good-hearted volunteer developer updates or replaces Zotero-OCR.

Many other document types—including rich-text documents (like your standard Microsoft Word document) and spreadsheets—can be saved as searchable PDFs. Saving a PDF copy will allow you to make most attachments searchable, if desired. If you also want to have access to the document in its native form, you can attach or link to both the PDF and its original file.

EPUB Features

The EPUB (Electronic Publication) format has become the most popular e-document format, due to its capacity to resize itself to whatever device it is on. Unlike PDFs, which can be hard to read on many smartphones, EPUBs can easily be read in the smaller formats. An EPUB version of this book is available from the Genohistory.com store, so you can view and mark it up. You can highlight, underline, and add notes to this format.

EPUBs are designed to reflow automatically to optimize a document's layout to the device and window in which it is displayed. They also allow you to alter fonts and their sizes, line height, and word and letter spacing to work best with your eyesight. With Zotero 7, EPUBs have become a fundamental part of the Zotero interface. While EPUBs cannot yet be imported with ZOTERO CONNECTOR, the CREATE PARENT ITEM option can be used to draw citation information from the EPUB's metadata, assuming it was built with metadata. Zotero hopes to make EPUBs importable through ZOTERO CONNECTOR soon.[1]

The EPUB will not initially have all the same annotation tools as a PDF. It will have highlights, underlines, and notes.

HTML/WEB SNAPSHOT FEATURES

Web snapshots are HTML captures of a web page at a moment in time. To activate these captures, you must select AUTOMATICALLY TAKE SNAPSHOTS WHEN CREATING ITEMS FROM WEB PAGES in the FILE HANDLING section in EDIT > SETTINGS > GENERAL. Zotero captures the snapshots when you use ZOTERO CONNECTOR to bring a web page into the database.

While PDFs can be attached with links to an external drive and annotated in the ZOTERO READER, web snapshots cannot. A snapshot, which is the HTML file captured from a webpage, must be stored inside Zotero to have annotations stored with it. Snapshots bring great value to researchers because they capture a website exactly as it was in a moment in time. If your publisher requires you to show images of a page you have cited for fact-checking, the snapshot does that for you. The fact that you can now annotate these files in Zotero 7 makes them even more valuable. You can mark up a webpage without having to convert it to a static PDF first. You can keep the website's original format, protecting your citation proof should a website or the text you cited within it be removed or changed.

---

[1] "Available for Beta Testing: Updated Reader with EPUB/Snapshot Support and New Annotation Types," Zotero Forums, August 7, 2023, https://forums.zotero.org/discussion/106716/available-for-beta-testing-updated-reader-with-epub-snapshot-support-and-new-annotation-types.

Snapshots will not initially have all the same annotation tools as a PDF. They will have highlights, underlines, and notes. The contents of snapshots are also searchable.

The snapshots take up space in your Zotero cloud storage, so you will want to get paid storage if you plan to use them consistently. Given how much of our information is drawn from web pages now, this new feature makes paid storage worth it, all by itself. In fact, after seventeen years of opting to keep my Zotero account free, I have finally signed up for unlimited storage because this feature stacks the benefits too deep to pass up for a few dimes a day.

ZOTERO READER SETTINGS

Reader

Open PDFs using   Zotero ⌄

Open EPUBs using   Zotero ⌄

Open snapshots using   Zotero ⌄

☐ Open files in new windows instead of tabs

Show tabs as   Creator - Year - Title ⌄

Ebook font: Georgia ⌄

☑ Enable automatic hyphenation

In EDIT > SETTINGS > GENERAL, the READER section contains options that control how the ZOTERO READER will function on your computer.

SETTING: OPEN USING

To determine how Zotero will handle the READER for PDFs, EPUBs, and HTML snapshots, go to EDIT > SETTINGS > GENERAL (READER section). First, you can choose whether you want these documents opened in the ZOTERO READER at all. Each document option defaults to ZOTERO, meaning that the document will open in the ZOTERO READER unless you manually override that option when opening it. The second option for all three document types is SYSTEM DEFAULT, which will open the document in whatever software program you have set in your computer system's program defaults for these file types. As a last option, you may map the document type to a reader program of your choice.

SETTING: OPEN FILES IN NEW WINDOWS INSTEAD OF TABS

If you keep the OPEN USING option set to ZOTERO, you can choose how it will be displayed. If you have deselected OPEN FILES IN NEW WINDOWS INSTEAD OF TABS, your document will open in a tab to the right of MY LIBRARY. It will have the full features available for each type, including a right-side panel that can display either the reference information for the document or the notes attached to the item (with all other notes available below it). The left pane displays all material that you underline, highlight, add, capture, draw, or type. Or, if you choose, it shows your table of contents or thumbnails of your PDF. The top toolbar contains all the tools to mark up and annotate the document, along with navigation and search tools.

If you choose instead to display the document in a separate window, you will be able to position and size the document in the way that most suits you. The window will display all the same features of the tabbed version, except for the right pane. You can display the reference and note information in the main window, which lies behind your freestanding document.

SETTING: SHOW TABS AS

This setting determines what Zotero will display on the READER tab and the window's title bar. This is helpful if you have more than a few documents open in your ZOTERO READER. You can set this in one of these three ways. Choose the option that has your most needed piece of information first:

- Title – Creator – Year
- Creator – Year – Title

- Filename

SETTING: EBOOK FONT

This setting allows you to choose the display font that works best for you in reading eBooks. You can select a style change here, not a size change. You can enlarge the text in your eBook using the Zoom controls.

EXERCISE 14. ANNOTATING A PDF IN ZOTERO READER

This exercise will use the MARKDOWN FORMATTING IN ZOTERO NOTES document in your sample data to get familiar with the ZOTERO READER, its workspace, and its functions.

STEP 1

Go to the SEARCH window on your main workspace toolbar and type "Markdown." Double-click on the PDF labeled BAKER – MARKDOWN FORMATTING IN ZOTERO NOTES. Your PDF should open in a tab in the ZOTERO READER. (If it opens in a separate window, instead, it will not allow use of the right pane for this exercise. Close the new window, go to EDIT > SETTINGS > GENERAL, and de-select OPEN FILES IN NEW WINDOWS INSTEAD OF TABS. Then, try again.)

STEP 2

If you do not see an active sidebar to the left of the document pane, click the TOGGLE SIDEBAR tool (1st element on the left) on the main READER toolbar. An empty ANNOTATIONS pane should be displayed on the left.

STEP 3

 Select the first sentence of the second paragraph in the main document—the one starting "You may happen upon some...." Zotero will present a COLOR BOX, for you to decide what color your highlights should be. Select YELLOW. The sentence should now have a yellow background. You should also see your first annotation showing up in the left pane.

STEP 4

If you do not see a sidebar to the right of your document, click the right-most button above the document, with the TOGGLE CONTEXT PANES tooltip label. An INFO section is probably in the right pane.

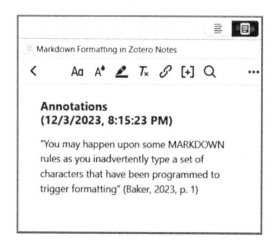

Any or all highlighted or underlined text can be pulled into an item note, becoming a summary of and link to all you considered important in the document.

STEP 5

To add a note, click on the NOTES button—the next-to-last button running down the right side of the sidebar. Click on the PLUS SIGN (+) next to ITEM NOTES in the right sidebar. (Widen the window or pane, if the + does not show.) Choose to ADD ITEM NOTE FROM ANNOTATIONS. This function pulls any annotations you have created into a single note, citing the source. It also links the text to the highlighted text in your document.

STEP 6

Find another sentence to mark—this time to underline. Click on the UNDERLINE button on the toolbar—two buttons to the right of the page number. Then select the text. It will be underlined in YELLOW, since that was the last color used. Right-click on the underlined text and change it to GREEN. Right-click again and choose ADD TO NOTE to write this text out to the same ITEM NOTE.

STEP 7

Close the current READER tab and return to MY LIBRARY. The document you just annotated will be a quick reference tool you might want to have handy whenever you are typing notes in Zotero. So, find it in your library and drag it to your QUICK REFERENCE collection. It will always be there if you need to know how to use the Markdown language to expedite the formatting of notes.

QUICK TIP: You can toggle between a SCROLLING state and a HAND state in your READER by using the lowercase letters S and H. In the SCROLLING state, your pointer device inserts a cursor in the displayed text. In the HAND state, you can drag the page up and down.

ZOTERO READER REFERENCE GUIDE

The ZOTERO READER's usefulness is expanded by tools and functions on the main menu, context menus, and toolbars. In the interest of being a "quick guide," I have not attempted to document every menu and button function in other parts of Zotero. But I am documenting the READER more thoroughly, as promised. It is new to many of us and has expanded Zotero's usefulness in phenomenal ways since Zotero 5, when I wrote *Zotero for Genealogy* and *The Zotero Solution*. And though we will not be describing the plugins in detail in this Quick Guide, plugins expand these features even further. Below are the tools and functions that come built-in with the ZOTERO READER. Some features work for all document types and others for specific ones. In brackets, you will see which types it works for.

Workspace Main Toolbar

Left Section

[ALL] Opens and closes the left pane.

[ALL] Zooms outward in the document view, making the text smaller and fitting more in the window.

[ALL] Zooms into the document, making the text larger.

[ALL] Expands or reduces the displayed text to fit the width of the pane.

[ALL] If you have moved through the document, this takes you back through that history.

[PDF, EPUB] Moves back a page in paginated documents and back a screen in scrolled documents.

[PDF, EPUB] Moves forward a page in paginated documents and forward a screen in scrolled documents.

8 | 194/206

[PDF, EPUB (paginated)] The editable number in the box represents the assigned page numbering for the section of your document. In some cases, it will be the same as the second number, which represents the actual page number. It will differ if the sections of a document begin page numbering over or if the document's page numbering starts at something other than 1. The third number is the total number of pages in the document.

MIDDLE SECTION

[ALL] Highlights text in a color from the available color palette. The marked text becomes an annotation in the left pane and can be written into child notes to the parent item.

[ALL] Underlines text in a color from the available color palette. The marked text becomes an annotation in the left pane and can be written into child notes to the parent item.

[ALL] Attaches "sticky notes" to the active document. The marked text becomes an annotation in the left pane and can be written into child notes to the parent item.

T

[PDF] Inserts a text box wherever the user desires. The marked text becomes an annotation in the left pane and can be written into child notes to the parent item. While the other text annotations can be linked from the child note to the place where the text originates in the document, this form of text cannot be linked.

[PDF] Captures the screen print of a selected area, which is then displayed as an annotation. This annotation cannot be inserted into a child note.

[PDF] Draws figures with a set of colors. This annotation cannot be inserted into a child note.

[PDF] Erases lines drawn with the drawing tool.

[ALL] Color palette, setting the highlighting, underlining, note color, or text box.

RIGHT SECTION

[ALL] Searches document for occurrence of the search string, going either forward or backward. Does not search the notes or annotations. They have a separate search window in the NOTES LIST.

[ALL] Item Reference. Shows reference information for the document's parent item.

[ALL] NOTES LIST/SINGLE VIEW. Lists all notes in the ITEM LIST, beginning with those that are attached to the parent item of the displayed document. When you select one, the pane shifts to a single view of the selected note.

LEFT PANE

This toolbar sits at the top of the left pane of the ZOTERO READER, creating three alternate views for this pane. The button with colors reversed indicates which pane view is active at present.

[PDF] Show thumbnails. Creates small images of each page in the PDF, allowing you to delete or rotate pages.

[ALL] Show Annotations. Displays an item for each markup or text annotation you have attached to the displayed document. Each item can be tagged, and some will allow comments to be added.

[ALL] Show Document Outline. Displays the table of contents. Double-click on items to expand to deeper levels of detail.

ZOTERO READER MENUS

These reader-specific functions appear in the main menu and are altered by whether you are in a PDF, EPUB, or snapshot view. Those marked with an asterisk are also available from the right-click context menu in documents.

FILE MENU

SAVE AS

[PDF] PDFs can be saved to a new place with a new name, if useful.

PRINT

[ALL] All three formats can be printed to a device or file.

SHOW IN LIBRARY

[ALL] This option will take you back to the ITEM LIST, to the parent item of the active document.

CLOSE

[ALL] This closes the active document's window or tab.

ROTATE PAGE LEFT

[PDF] Selected PDF pages can be rotated counterclockwise in 90-degree increments.

ROTATE PAGE RIGHT

[PDF] Selected PDF pages can be rotated clockwise in 90-degree increments.

VIEW MENU

HAND TOOL

[PDF] When activated, your movements of the mouse become dragging motions to move your PDF document around.

VERTICAL SCROLLING

[PDF] This option allows you to roll through your PDF's pages in an up-and-down motion using the up- and down-arrow keys.

HORIZONTAL SCROLLING

[PDF] This option allows you to roll through your PDF's pages in a side-to-side motion using the right- and left-arrow keys.

WRAPPED SCROLLING

[PDF] This option activates both vertical and horizontal scrolling but scrolls by whole pages per keystroke.

SCROLLED

[EPUB] EPUBs should be scrolled if images or tables are in the text. This allows you to smoothly scroll up and down with the arrow keys.

PAGINATED

[EPUB] With this option an EPUB will scroll a page at a time. If there are images or tables in the text, they might be shrunk to a small enough size to fit on a single page.

NO SPREADS

[PDF, EPUB] This limits the document view to a single page at a time, rather than a two-page spread. Spreads are only relevant to EPUBs that support reflowing text and are set to be paginated, rather than scrollable.

ODD SPREADS

[PDF, EPUB] This creates a two-page spread, with the first page falling on the odd page. Spreads are only relevant to EPUBs that support reflowing text and are set to be paginated, rather than scrollable.

EVEN SPREADS

[PDF] This creates a two-page spread, with the first page falling on the even page.

ZOOM IN*

[ALL] This option zooms into the document. In the case of a PDF, the page design remains intact and will begin to move beyond the edges of your view. With EPUB and HTML documents, the words will begin to wrap.

ZOOM OUT*

[ALL] This option moves out from the document, making the text smaller and fitting more in the view.

RESET ZOOM*

[EPUB, HTML] This option restores the document to its default text size.

AUTOMATICALLY RESIZE*

[PDF] This option returns a PDF to its original view.

ZOOM TO PAGE WIDTH*

[PDF] This option sets a PDF to fit its full-page width in the view.

ZOOM TO PAGE HEIGHT

[PDF] This option sets a PDF to fit its full-page height in the view.

SPLIT HORIZONTALLY*

[PDF, EPUB] This option splits the screen across the middle, allowing you to look at two views of the document simultaneously, one stacked on the other.

SPLIT VERTICALLY*

[ALL] This option splits the screen from top to bottom, allowing you to look at two views of the document simultaneously, side by side.

GO MENU

FIRST PAGE

[PDF, EPUB] Moves to the first page in the active document.

LAST PAGE

[PDF, EPUB] Moves to the last page in the active document.

FORWARD/NEXT PAGE

[Alt+->]*
(EPUB) The shortcut moves forward through an EPUB file by increments that are roughly the size of a page.

Backward/Previous Page
[Alt+<-]*
(EPUB) The shortcut moves backward through an EPUB file by increments that are roughly the size of a page.

ZOTERO READER TAB CONTEXT MENU FUNCTIONS

The following functions are available when you right-click on a ZOTERO READER tab. The last two functions also appear when you right-click on the COLLECTIONS tab at the left.

SHOW IN LIBRARY

Reactivates the ITEM LIST pane, selecting the parent item of the document whose tab was clicked.

MOVE TAB

Allows you to move a tab to the start, the end, or to a new window. (Tabs can also be dragged and dropped into new locations.)

DUPLICATE TAB

Repeats the activation of the current tab.

CLOSE

Closes the current tab.

CLOSE OTHER TABS

Closes all but the current tab.

REOPEN CLOSED TABS

Reopens the last tab(s) closed.

A short menu pops up immediately when you select text in any of the three document types.

[COLORS]

[ALL] When text is selected originally, a bar with the available highlight colors will appear, allowing you to rapidly create highlights in the chosen color.

ADD TO NOTE

[ALL] Once you have opened a child note attached to this document's parent item in your right pane, you can transfer the selected text to it. It will be automatically linked to the selected text if drawn from highlighted or underlined text. You can quickly find it again by clicking anywhere in the note's text and using the SHOW ON PAGE context menu.

Another menu appears when you right-click in the main text. This context menu offers functions described in the main menu section.

The following functions are available when you right-click an existing annotation or click the selection button (three dots) on an annotation item in the left pane of the ZOTERO READER.

ADD TO NOTE

[ALL] Once you have opened a child note attached to this document's parent item in your right pane, you can transfer the annotation's text to it. It will be automatically linked to the selected text. You can quickly find the annotation again by clicking anywhere in the note's text and using the SHOW ON PAGE context menu.

[COLORS]

Alter the color of an annotation's highlights, underlining, sticky notes, or (for PDFs) text or drawings.

SIZE

[Drawings only] You can change the thickness of a drawn line.

EDIT PAGE NUMBER...

[Selection button, PDF only] A PDF's page numbering might not match the page numbering of the original document. This option lets you edit the starting page number for the individual annotation, the page, or the page and all following pages.

EDIT ANNOTATION TEXT

[Selection button only] When you highlight or underline text in the READER, the affected text will be extracted into an annotation. This function allows you to edit or add to the text.

DELETE

This function removes whatever has been created in an annotation, including the highlights, underlines, drawings, and notes.

QUICK TIP: Most annotation types can be tagged with the same base of tags used in the main Zotero database. Some allow you to add COMMENTS, as well. TAGS and COMMENTS are searchable and can be filtered in the main search engine.

---

8. CITATIONS, BIBLIOGRAPHIES, AND WORD PROCESSORS

In graduate school, I had to write numerous research papers, and finally a dissertation. The U.S. history field generally required the use of a publishing style guide called the *Chicago Manual of Style (CMOS)* or a student version we referred to as "Turabian."[1] *CMOS*, with one-thousand-plus pages of rules and guidelines, was intimidatingly thorough. Once Zotero entered the picture, though, I lost my dread of citations and bibliographies. Zotero's WORD PROCESSOR PLUGINS create them for me.

Most research fields need such a tool for the writing of formal articles, books, and research reports. Zotero's plugins for Word for Windows and other popular word processors will take much pain out of it for anyone using standard publishing styles. Approximately 10,000 citation styles and style variants are available through Zotero to support most academic fields and many research disciplines beyond academia. Zotero also offers very quick ways to draw formatted citations, bibliographies, and notes from its library into most text-based tools, including email and blog software.

A NOTE TO GENEALOGISTS: See Chapter 9 for a section that describes the absence of the style documented in *Evidence Explained* style in Zotero and suggests the best workaround using *CMOS*.

SETTING UP THE WORD PROCESSING PLUGIN

Zotero automatically installs the plugins for Microsoft Word for Windows, Mac, and LibreOffice. Google Docs becomes Zotero-enabled when you add your ZOTERO CONNECTION extension to a Chrome, Firefox, Edge, or Safari browser. It also must have the desktop version of Zotero installed on your computer to work.

---

[1] Kate L. Turabian et al., A Manual for Writers of Research Papers, Theses, and Dissertations, Ninth Edition: Chicago Style for Students and Researchers, Ninth edition (Chicago London: University of Chicago Press, 2018).

ZOTERO MENU

You should see the plugin set up in your word processor if the installation was successful. It will appear as a menu item across the top of your word processor's workspace. The tools might appear as a submenu or as a toolbar, depending on your word processor.

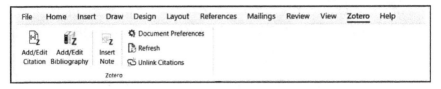

If your word processor has Zotero installed, a menu item will appear near the HELP menu on your word processor.

For our instructional purposes here, we will use Microsoft Word for Windows as the model, but the functions should be similar for most supported word processors. Check Zotero's WORD PROCESSOR PLUGINS[2] page for information about setting up or troubleshooting the plugin with your chosen word processor, if you encounter problems or have questions.

ZOTERO TOOLS IN YOUR WORD PROCESSOR

You have research stored in Zotero now and your word processing add-on set up. Next, we will start using the add-on in your word-processing software. Open that software, create a new blank document, and examine the tools Zotero has installed for you.

In Word for Windows, you should see a Zotero tab on your menu bar, probably the last item before your HELP menu, unless you have added other customizations to your software. Click on the tab, and a set of tools will appear beneath the menu bar.

With these tools, you will be able to pull citation data from Zotero and format it as footnotes or endnotes. When you have created these notes, you can then use the tools to create a bibliography. The data you import remains "dynamic." Let's say you find later that you had something incorrect in Zotero. You correct it in

---

[2] https://www.zotero.org/support/word_processor_integration

Zotero, then you can refresh your document, automatically replacing the incorrect information throughout the entire document with your corrected Zotero information.

QUICK TIP: As long as your document remains private to you, the dynamic setup is workable. But you will not want to send the document to your publisher or professor or genealogy client with the Zotero fields still connected throughout it. The UNLINK CITATIONS field on the toolbar can disconnect your document from Zotero. Do this ONLY to a copy of the document. Always keep your original document connected to Zotero for future use.

DOCUMENT PREFERENCES

Before you begin to work with your new document, you will want to make sure you have set your preferences. Click on DOCUMENT PREFERENCES on your Zotero plugin toolbar.

You are offered the following options:

CITATION STYLE

Unless you have a specific style requirement other than *CMOS*, select CHICAGO MANUAL OF STYLE 17TH EDITION (FULL NOTE)—or a newer version, if available. The MANAGE STYLES... link opens Zotero's SETTINGS > CITE where more styles can be accessed or edited.

LANGUAGE

Choose the language your citations will use.

DISPLAY CITATION AS

Choose whether your citations are to be footnotes or endnotes. A footnote displays a citation at the bottom of the page containing the information the citation supports. An endnote appears at the end of a chapter, report, or book—gathered with all the other citations.

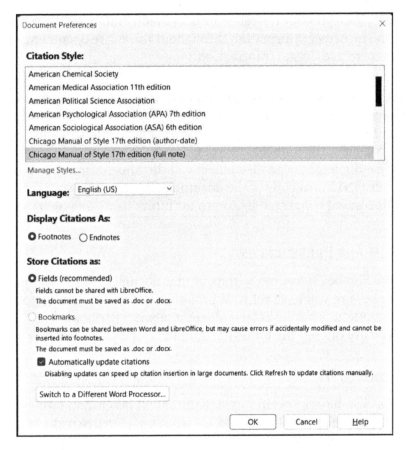

*The DOCUMENT PREFERENCES determine how your
citations will function.*

STORE CITATION AS

Choose whether you want the citation to be stored as a field or a
bookmark. In most cases, you will want to choose FIELD. This creates a dynamic reference in your word processor, which can be updated if citation information changes in Zotero. If you plan to
move your document over to LibreOffice at any point, you will
need to choose BOOKMARK. (Test thoroughly before transferring
any document with Zotero citations to another word processing
tool. Transfer a copy, not the original.)

Activate this option if you want your document automatically and instantly to pull in changes from Zotero, altering citations you have already entered. With each change you make, Zotero will be searching the whole document for other references to the same source. As your document grows large, you might prefer to turn this off, to speed up your entry of new citations. If you deselect this option, you will want to click REFRESH on the Zotero toolbar occasionally to manually update all fields in your document.

THE STATUS OF URLS

If you have input a URL address in the reference information of an item, it will always be included in a citation unless these two conditions are in place:

- Select the Include URLs in Paper Articles in References in Zotero's Edit > Settings > Cite, under the Citation Options.

- The Pages field in your item's reference information must contain a page number or range.

CREATING CITATIONS IN YOUR DOCUMENT

You must have Zotero open on your desktop for your word processor to know where to apply your changes. The Zotero plugin for Word makes citation creation remarkably easy. When you have written something that requires a citation, you click the ADD/EDIT CITATION icon to bring up a QUICK FORMAT bar that interfaces with your Zotero database. The first visible Zotero record will be the one that is currently selected in Zotero at the moment. Given that you probably are consulting this record as you write the document, you may only need to press ENTER to fill in the desired citation information.

If you do not see your desired record at the top of the QUICK FORMAT list, you can find it by typing in enough text for Zotero to pull it into the window—along with any other items that are a match. You will highlight the source record, then click ENTER to create the citation. Or just after you select the record, type in a comma and page number, to add that to the citation.

EXERCISE 15. CREATE A CITATION

PREREQUISITE: EXERCISE 3

In this exercise, you will experiment with adding a citation to your empty document.

STEP 1

Open Zotero on your desktop and open your word processor to a new document for experimentation.

STEP 2

Type this sentence into your document: "Insert text here."

STEP 3

Click on the Zotero toolbar and then choose ADD/EDIT CITATION to create your citation.

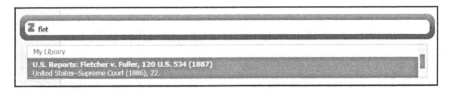

Type a string of text from your source's author or title to bring it into the drop-down list for selection.

STEP 4

A red rectangular bar will appear on your screen. Begin to type "Fletcher" and select the option displayed in the rectangle shown. Click ENTER. The Zotero plugin will insert a superscripted number at the spot where you were in the document. It will create a footnote at the bottom of your page (or at the chapter's end, if you've chosen endnotes) that looks like this:

Zotero's word processor plugin draws reference data from the Zotero database and formats it into the proper citation and reference style in the document.

STEP 5

Keep this document open for the next exercise or save it where you can bring it back up.

ADDING MULTIPLE ZOTERO CITATIONS

Enter multiple search strings to create a footnote with more than one citation.

You will often find that you need several Zotero items to support a point you have made in your document. To create multiple citations under a single footnote, click ADD/EDIT CITATIONS from your Zotero toolbar. Type in the search string for the first record you want to cite and select the correct one from Zotero's list. Then, rather than clicking ENTER, type your SPACEBAR and another search string. Repeat this until all citations are included for this one footnote Zotero will separate the citations by a semicolon, as is common practice for the *CMOS* style.

EDITING A CITATION

As you create citations, you might find that you have pulled the incorrect one, or that you need to add further information to make the citation complete. Or you may realize that you had the information incorrect in Zotero to begin with. You may easily correct all of them, by one of several methods described below.

CHOOSING A DIFFERENT ZOTERO RECORD

If you chose the wrong Zotero record, you could do one of two things. First, simply delete the superscripted number in your text, which will delete the footnote or endnote. Then you go through the steps again to add a new record. Or you can click anywhere in the footnote and click ADD/EDIT CITATION on your Zotero toolbar. The Zotero bar will appear again, with the selected record displayed. Backspace to remove the citation you chose, then type in the valid text to find the one you prefer.

ADDING DETAIL TO A CITATION

To add a prefix, suffix, or page numbering, click on the asset's title in the Zotero bar in Microsoft Word.

When you click on a source you have selected from the Zotero search bar, a window will appear offering fields to add useful or required information to your citation. You can number or label things like items in a series, pages, chapters, and many other options. You can insert any text you want to add before or after the reference information in the prefix and suffix fields. You can also choose to omit the AUTHOR, and you can open Zotero to the reference item, allowing you to alter the information you have stored there.

In situations where you have more than one citation, adding punctuation at the end of the SUFFIX field of the first citation will use the punctuation between the two items. Without any punctuation at the end of the SUFFIX field, Zotero will insert a semicolon or whatever divider is common in your chosen style.

If you try instead to simply type extra information into the Zotero-created footnote, you will disable the dynamic update of the field. Changes to the data in your Zotero database will not update and attempts to edit the citation using your Zotero plugin will bring up a blank window.

Shortcuts to Add a Page Number to Your Citation

You can add a page number by typing it after you have selected the item and brought it into the Zotero search window. Click ENTER to set it into the footnotes.

The plugin will only accept a number after the comma. If you type letters, it will assume you want to add a second citation. When you complete your number, and press ENTER, it will place the number in the appropriate page number format for your citation's style and item type.

If you decide to add a page number after you have already created the citation, click in the citation text and click the ADD/EDIT CITATION button on your Zotero toolbar. The selection bar will reappear with your citation field displayed. Type the page number after it, and Zotero will fold it into the field with a period after it. Click ENTER to reformat the citation with the page number in it. You may also expedite your footnote entry by typing the search text, a space, and the page number before selecting the Zotero footnote. When you make your selection, the page number will be stored.

Subsequent Citations

The plugin will determine how to handle subsequent citations of the same source, depending on your chosen style. In *CMOS*, citing the same source twice in a row will be handled with the author's last name and a new page number, if different. If the same source is cited near the original, *CMOS* attempts to abbreviate the second citation, putting only enough for you to identify what the source is. It is here that it uses the SHORT TITLE from your Zotero database. The plugin will also use the SHORT TITLE in place of a page number if you do not identify the page.

INSERTING NOTES

The INSERT NOTE item on the plugin toolbar will pull the entire text of a note from your Zotero database into your document.

CREATING A BIBLIOGRAPHY

Zotero's plugin for Microsoft Word offers a very simple way to create a bibliography of all sources cited within the document. Go to the spot in the document where you want the bibliography to appear. Click on the ADD/EDIT BIBLIOGRAPHY button on the Zotero toolbar, and the bibliography will be inserted at the spot. Zotero will format it according to your chosen style. Please note that it does not create hyperlinks from URL addresses. This is something that can be done with macros in some word processing software after you have inserted the bibliographical data.

VIEWING ZOTERO BIBLIOGRAPHIC FORMATS

As you prepare to enter reference information into Zotero to cite a source, sometimes the choice of an ITEM TYPE will be simple. Sometimes, you are not sure which is best for a given reference. Your SAMPLE DATA can help you in your decisions. Look at the folder called ZOTERO BIBLIOGRAPHIC FORMATS. It contains filler data in every field of every ITEM TYPE. If you want to see how the various fields are displayed in a bibliographic entry or footnote, you can do it in one of two ways:

SETTINGS STYLE PREVIEW

This option allows you to see how your footnote and reference will look in one of the most common styles. While the desired format item is selected in your ITEM LIST, select EDIT > SETTINGS > CITE, then click on STYLE PREVIEW at the bottom of the screen. A window appears with your chosen item's data mapped to multiple different styles. Click REFRESH if you are not seeing the data.

PASTE BIBLIOGRAPHIC DATA INTO NOTE

Another way (my preferred way) to use these samples is to right-click on the item and choose CREATE BIBLIOGRAPHY FROM ITEM. You can choose the style, decide whether to capture a bibliographic reference or a footnote and choose the output format. I choose to output to the clipboard, then add a child note to the item. I paste the format into the note—often doing both the bibliographic entry and footnote.

You can experiment with the sample formatting items—adding and leaving out things until you have things looking the way you want them to. That becomes your guide for how to do your actual data entry.

Bibliography

Farley, S. E. "Popular Prejudices." *Godey's Lady's Book, and Ladies' American Magazine*, May 1842.

Kte'pi, Bill. "Presentism and Cultural Bias." *Presentism & Cultural Bias – Research Starters Sociology*, 9/1/2021 2021, 1-4.

Legacy Tree Genealogists. "How Social and Historical Context Can Guard Against Presentism." *Legacy Tree* (blog), October 16, 2020. https://www.legacytree.com/blog/social-historical-context.

Posz, CG, Darcie Hinds. "Baggage: Presentism from Both Sides of the Fence." *APG Quarterly* 29, no. 1 (March 2014): 24-.

Wilson, Jeffrey R. "Historicizing Presentism: Toward the Creation of a Journal of the Public Humanities – Profession." *MLA Profession* 2019, no. Spring (July 27, 2019). https://profession.mla.org/historicizing-presentism-toward-the-creation-of-a-journal-of-the-public-humanities/.

Zotero will create a bibliography for you at the desired spot in your document.

QUICK COPY CITATIONS AND BIBLIOGRAPHIES

You can use copy-and-paste or drag-and-drop functions to quickly create the formatted information you need to cite a source, send a colleague a set of sources related to a subject of interest, or any number of other scenarios. Without the word processor plugin, however, the citations and bibliographic elements you create in a document will not be linked back to Zotero. If you later correct an error in a Zotero item, it will not automatically correct it in your document.

In EDIT > SETTINGS > EXPORT, you can set your preferred citation style for creating quick citation and bibliography entries. You can also set your preferred language and flag the text to be copied as HTML text if needed.

QUICK COPY BIBLIOGRAPHIES

To create a quick bibliography, select multiple items from the ITEM LIST and drag and drop them into a blank document, email, or other text-based software. Or, if you prefer, you can use EDIT > COPY BIBLIOGRAPHY (CTRL+SHIFT+C), then paste the text into your document. The data will be reformatted and pasted wherever you drop the data. Here is the output of dragging six items from my ITEM LIST:

Abrams, Ulysses Huey, and Mattie Sandford Johnson. *A History of Early Bibb County, Alabama, 1820-1870*. Huntsville, Ala.: M.S. Johnson, 1981.

Alabama Watchman. Cahawba, Ala: A. Parsons, 1820.

Boyd, Gregory A. 1960-(Gregory Alan). *Family Maps of Bibb County, Alabama*. Norman, OK: Arphax Publishing Company, 2006.

Davidson, Henry Damon. "Inching Along"; or, The Life and Work of an Alabama Farm Boy, an Autobiography. Nashville, Tenn.: National Publication Company, 1944.

England, Flora D. Index to Book A, Minutes of the Probate Court, Bibb County, Alabama. Marion, Ala, 1965.

Hobson, Mike. "Historic Ellison Estate Tract Sold | The Bibb Voice." Accessed September 5, 2019. https://www.bibbvoice.com/2019/03/26/historic-ellison-estate-tract-sold/.

Unlike using the ZOTERO WORD PROCESSING plugin, the URL addresses are automatically turned into active hyperlinks. Regardless of what order Zotero displays the selected items in the ITEM LIST, they will be alphabetized in the document receiving the bibliographic text.

QUICK COPY CITATIONS

To take a Zotero item or a group of them and create citations in a document, you will make minor changes to the instructions for a bibliography. As you drag a group of items, hold down the SHIFT key before you drop them into the document. Or you can copy using EDIT > COPY CITATION (CTRL+SHIFT+A) and paste the text into the document. Zotero combines all elements into a single paragraph—supporting one footnote or endnote in your document. A group citation will paste looking something like this:

William Bingley, *Travels in North America* (London: Printed for Harvey and Darton, 1821); "Natchez," *Mississippi State Gazette*, April 29, 1820, VIII: 18; "From the Richmond Compiler," *Alexandria Gazette*, July 6, 1818, XIX: 5271.

CREATE CITATION/BIBLIOGRAPHY

You can create both bibliography and citation text by right-clicking on the Zotero item and choosing CREATE BIBLIOGRAPHY FROM ITEM. This will display a window with selections you can make to refine what you will output in your external document.

When you choose multiple items to be output as NOTES, they will be output as a paragraph of citations, separated by semicolons, rather than as a list. The bibliographic elements will be output just as the drag-and-drop action does—in a list.

QUICK COPY NOTES

Notes you have created in Zotero—whether independent or child notes of parent items—can be dragged and dropped into text-processing software, just as the citation and bibliographic data can. Or if you prefer to use the menu or keyboard shortcuts, they are at EDIT > COPY NOTES (CTRL+SHIFT+C).

EXERCISE 16. INSERT ZOTERO NOTES INTO DOCUMENT

PREREQUISITE: EXERCISE 3, 15

In this exercise, you will replace text created in the previous exercise with a note in your ZOTERO 7 SAMPLE DATA.

STEP 1

Return to the document you created in the previous exercise.

STEP 2

In the main body of the document, select the words you typed: "Insert text here." Do not select the footnote superscripted number at the end of the text.

STEP 3

In Zotero, click on the subcollection ZOTERO 7 SAMPLE DATA. In the ITEM LIST, find the document titled "U.S. Reports: Fletcher v. Fuller, 120 U.S. 534 (1887)." It should have a note attached to it, beginning with the words, "Defendants in ejectment..." Click on the note, select it all, and press the keystroke combination CTRL+SHIFT+C (or choose EDIT > COPY NOTE from your menu).

STEP 4

Return to your document and paste the new text over the selected text. (In Word, the shortcut is CTRL+V.) The words "Insert text here" should be replaced with a lengthy paragraph containing the text of the note you copied. It will also insert an extra paragraph marker, pushing the footnote symbol down a line. You can press your BACKSPACE key to correct that.

9. MISCELLANEOUS

PLUGINS

A constantly expanding set of independently created Zotero plugins enhance its usefulness, beyond what is already offered with the ZOTERO CONNECTOR and the word-processing plugins. Some are remarkable, well-maintained, and diligently supported by their makers. Some are less so. I have mentioned a few. Future Quick Guides will illuminate some of the most valuable plugins, offering creative ways to use them in your research workflow.

Meanwhile, I will name a few of the ones that I consider too good to wait for and connect you with the websites where they can be downloaded. I will offer the basic instructions for adding plugins, also. Be aware that these plugins are being developed by a worldwide group of programmers. The instructions are usually created in the programmer's native language. When you see language you do not recognize, right-click on the text and instruct the system to translate the page to your language, if the option is available.

PERSONAL FAVORITES AMONG ZOTERO PLUGINS

ADD-ON MARKET FOR ZOTERO[1] is a new plugin that keeps track of the currently available plugins for Zotero, facilitates their installation, and manages your system's updates when a plugin has changed. This will hopefully give us all a more up-to-date list of what is available than we have had previously. Once you have manually installed this plugin, you will rarely need to install other plugins manually.

See the next major section for instructions for a manual installation. You will need to exit Zotero and come back in to activate the plugin. Once activated, a puzzle-piece icon will appear on the toolbar above the ITEM LIST, just left of the SEARCH box. Click on it to bring up a window of plugins and information about them.

---

[1] https://github.com/syt2/zotero-addons#readme

Right-click on one to INSTALL it or to get more information from
its HOMEPAGE.

BETTER NOTES FOR ZOTERO[2] is a remarkable tool for drawing together the insights of multiple reference sources to make a cohesive point or series of points. It has a mechanism to create
template documents for the many of us who like to consistently extract and apply information across resources.

ACTIONS AND TAGS FOR ZOTERO[3] is a very new plugin that replaces
the Zotero 6-and earlier ZUTILO tool many considered vital to
Zotero. This new plugin does just about everything ZUTILO did and
more. It's a utility file that handles numerous things like creating
links between Zotero items, applying tags to batches of items, and
many other things. It allows you to create shortcuts to set things in
motion and lets some scripts run when a certain action happens.
For example, you can tell it to add an UNREAD tag to a new PDF
when it is added to Zotero. If you have applicable programming
skills, you can also alter the scripts to tailor functions to your
needs.

MANUALLY INSTALLING PLUGINS

You might, on rare occasions, need to manually install plugins, after you install the ADD-ON MARKET FOR ZOTERO tool. There are two
vital things to look for as you download a plugin from GITHUB for
Zotero. First, you want to view its README page. This describes the
program and offers usage instructions. The other thing will be an
installation file, which ends with the XPI extension. Download the
XPI file to your computer and follow any instructions the online
documentation offers. Plugins are installed and activated in Zotero
through the TOOLS > ADD-ONS menu, through its settings button
(gear icon). After installation, you might need to exit Zotero and
come back in to activate components of your new plugins.

---

[2] https://github.com/windingwind/zotero-better-notes/blob/master/RE-
ADME.md
[3] https://github.com/windingwind/zotero-actions-tags/blob/master/RE-
ADME.md

USING EVIDENCE STYLE WITH ZOTERO

The Evidence Style (ES) was developed by Elizabeth Shown Mills and is documented in *Evidence Explained: Citing History Sources from Artifacts to Cyberspace* (2024—4th ed.). It covers a substantial breadth and complexity of multilayered research sources often overlooked by most academic styles. Some genealogical organizations prefer it for published work, certification efforts, and client reports. Most will also accept the University of Chicago's *Manual of Style (CMOS)*. I recommend a hybrid approach to get the most of two brilliant tools.

Zotero does not offer a specific ES format, due to the data complexity of the ES concept of "layering." ES incorporates the evidentiary chain of custody of sources from an original form to a derivative copy. Unfortunately, any attempt to structure such a variable chain into discrete data fields would likely bloat the data tables for the rest of the world's styles supported by Zotero—and there are more than ten thousand variations to serve. However, this does not rule out ES-informed citations created in Zotero.

You can bring Zotero and ES into harmony by capturing ES's *intent* with minor departures in syntax and sequence. The templates added in the 4th edition of *Evidence Explained* make this much simpler to do than it was with earlier versions.

I plan to create a citation guide in *The Genohistory Quick Guides Series* that will describe the Zotero-ES combination in more detail. But most of what you need to capture ES-informed citations using Zotero can be summed up here:

- Once every few years, read the extraordinary introductory chapters in *Evidence Explained* (4th edition or later) to refresh yourself on the intent of ES and why good citations matter so much.

- Trust Mills's assertion that "citation is an art, not a science." Put the *value* of your citation above fundamentalist adherence to what Mills always intended as a guide, not a mandate.[4]

---

[4] Elizabeth Shown Mills, *Evidence Explained: Citing History Sources from Artifacts to Cyberspace*, 4th ed. (Baltimore, MD: Genealogical Publishing Co, 2024), 47. Quoted material used with permission of the author.

- Trust that most publishers will accept valuable and *consistently* formatted citations and references. Be consistent in your use of Zotero to incorporate ES.

- Use *CMOS* style in Zotero to get as close to ES as possible. In many cases, you will find the two identical.

- In preparation for the rare publisher who demands perfect ES syntax, capture the page number from *Evidence Explained* as you capture the citation data in Zotero. (I put something like EE4: 115 in the EXTRA field to indicate page 115 in the 4th edition.) Then, go back before publication to perfect the syntax in your finished document. Even if this publisher never comes along, capturing the ES page number is good practice for future reference.

- Use the LOC IN ARCHIVE field in Zotero to capture the ES layers when needed. This field can hold all the text you will need and allows you to create italicized phrases within it, as you can do with titles.[5]

- Ask yourself, "Based on this citation, will my reader be able to (1) find this source, if findable, and (2) evaluate the probable reliability and value of the source?"

AN ES-INFORMED CITATION IN ZOTERO

Template 10 in the 4th Edition of *Evidence Explained* uses this citation:

1. Christian County, Kentucky, Will Book A: 46–47, Thomas Wadlington estate inventory, undated, filed December 1803; imaged, "Kentucky Probate Records, 1727–1990," *FamilySearch* (https://www.familysearch.org/search/collection/1875188: accessed 1 October 2023) > Christian > Will Records Index 1797–1811, Vol. A > images 35–36 of 137; citing "county courthouses, Kentucky."[6]

You can create this variant in Zotero:

---

[5] See the Titles section in Chapter 2 for information about formatting fields.
[6] Mills, 128.

1. Christian County, Kentucky, "Will Book A [46-47, Thomas Wadlington Estate Inventory]" (n.d.), filed December 1803; imaged, "Kentucky Probate Records, 1727–1990," > Christian > Will Records Index 1797–1811. Vol. A > images 35-36 of 137; citing "county courthouses, Kentucky," Family Search, https://www.familysearch.org/search/collection /1875188.

The information can be set up in Zotero in this way:

Item Type	Manuscript
Title	Will Book A [46-47, Thomas Wadlington Estate Inventory]
Author	Christian County, Kentucky
Date	n.d.
Archive	FamilySearch
Loc. in Archive	filed December 1803; imaged, "Kentucky Probate Records, 1727–1990," > Christian > Will Records Index 1797–1811. Vol. A > images 35-36 of 137; citing "county courthouses, Kentucky"
URL	https://www.familysearch.org/search/collection /1875188
Accessed	9/30/2023

Zotero stores the accessed date but follows *CMOS* standards in eliminating it from the footnote. If you prefer to include it, type it in the LOC IN ARCHIVE field instead. Zotero also defaults quotation marks around anything typed into the Title field for the manuscript and document field types. If you do not want the quotation marks to appear in a published document with this source, place a symbol before and after the title. Let's say you use an asterisk. When your document is complete, search and replace "* and *" with nothing throughout. The remainder of the information is intact, though with a slightly different syntax.

STORED OR LINKED ATTACHMENTS — IN-DEPTH CONSIDERATIONS

If you are new to Zotero and uncertain whether to store or link to attachments, here are the variables to consider:

COST CONSIDERATIONS

If you choose to link to attachments in external locations, the 300 MB of free Zotero cloud space can last a very long time—assuming you are not pasting images into your notes or automatically downloading PDF and web snapshot files through ZOTERO CONNECTOR.

I used Zotero for many years, accumulating approximately 8,000 items and taking up only 32% of my free Zotero storage. Linked attachments made sense for my circumstances in graduate school and stuck with me after that mostly because I was used to it. In recent years, Zotero has become the core of more and more of what I do each day. And its features keep growing richer. I now operate with a hybrid of linked and stored attachments.

If you need to keep this a free product, you will find Zotero quite useful without storing your attachments. The choice to keep the product free will cost you more time, and only you know if you can afford that.

For some, you can afford the money more than the time. At present, Zotero offers 2 GB of storage for $20 a year or 6 GB for $60. Storing your attachments with the unlimited option costs $10 per month, or $120 per year—a very reasonable investment for anyone who is growing knowledge assets at a high level.

It is also important to note that storage subscriptions are a key funding source for the amazing Zotero team.

TIME CONSIDERATIONS

The stored attachments are considerably more convenient to a busy researcher than linked attachments, especially when using the ZOTERO CONNECTOR on a website that automatically downloads the PDF with the reference data, like JSTOR. With a press of a button on a webpage, Zotero creates the item, fills in all the reference information, attaches the PDF, and renames it for consistency, according to your specifications. There is no decision to make about where to store the PDF. Zotero creates a folder, deposits it there, and creates the links from the Zotero software to the attachment.

With a linked attachment coming from the same JSTOR page, ZOTERO CONNECTOR would create the item and fill in the reference information. But you would need to go back to the JSTOR page to download the PDF and choose where you want to keep it on your computer. Once there, you can rename it, if its default name doesn't suit your standards. Then you can drag it onto the Zotero reference item, holding down the CTRL and SHIFT keys before dropping it there, which creates a linked, rather than stored attachment.

I have done my linked attachments this way several thousand times without complaint. It is much faster than many other options, especially photocopying an article, creating a folder, creating an index card with bibliographic information, and the rigamarole that we once considered normal.

However, if time is your most limited resource, Zotero's storage can be well worth the investment.

SPACE CONSIDERATIONS

Attachments take up space—as they accumulate, a lot of space. Even one file can be a monster: I have a single map that is half a gigabyte in size. Storing attachments in the Zotero database will not free up space on your computer. Whether your attachments are stored or linked, they reside on your computer or in external storage, like Dropbox.

Zotero's online storage holds a *copy* of your data—not the main data itself. It is a perpetually updated snapshot of your data for your convenience, especially in syncing across multiple computers or offering remote access. At times the attachment file will exist first on your hard drive, before being stored in Zotero. In such a case, the original file might remain on your hard drive. So you will want to get rid of the original document if space needs to be freed.

With either arrangement, you need to also arrange for a secure backup regularly to a safe off-site location, as you should be doing for all information you value. See Zotero's documentation on BACKING UP YOUR ZOTERO DATA[7] for information.

Space considerations are roughly equivalent for linked and stored attachments. I recommend you store external linked documents in cloud storage, even if it is not Zotero's arrangement. Your data will likely be protected and backed up in your cloud solution, and you can access it when you are using Zotero on a computer other than your own.

REMOTE ACCESS

I rarely find myself separated from my laptop on planned research trips. But on the occasions when I find an hour to pop into an archive unexpectedly, it would be a great time-saver to have my entire library of attachments at my fingertips, using an archive's public computer.

Zotero's reference items and notes can be accessed through its online WEB LIBRARY at Zotero.org anywhere you have internet access. Attachments other than PDFs, EPUBs, and HTML snapshots behave differently through this remote access than they do on your computer with the desktop software. Stored attachments can be downloaded from the WEB LIBRARY when you are away from your computer. Linked attachments, on the other hand, cannot be viewed through Zotero's WEB LIBRARY when you are away from your computer, though it will show you that the attachment exists and what it is named.

If you keep your linked attachments in cloud storage of some kind, you will be able to get to the attachments and edit them by that means, if you know where you stored them. It is best to organize your externally linked files systematically—preferably in a similar order to how you organize information in Zotero.

---

[7] https://www.zotero.org/support/zotero_data#backing_up_your_zotero_data

Group Work

Zotero allows you to create groups to share libraries at ZOTERO.ORG/GROUPS.[8] If you plan to set up a group, allowing others to view and edit your work, you cannot use linked attachments in the group library. Links would be broken by group members inevitably. The person who establishes the group needs to have Zotero's storage option. Other group members do not have to have it, but any attachments they bring into the group library will count against the group leader's storage limits. I recommend any group leader who allows others to add items to the group library should opt for the unlimited storage option.

You may store your attachments in a shared environment like Google Drive and use a URL link, rather than Zotero's linked attachment method. However, any members with the power to edit the group library may attach documents.

Editing HTML Snapshot Documents

With Release 7, as discussed, Zotero has added a feature that makes paid storage a must-have for me. Zotero can save a snapshot of a webpage as you capture it with ZOTERO CONNECTOR. In this way, you document what a web page said at a precise time. It becomes your "wayback machine," in essence.

The wonderful new READER feature, with its ability to mark up and annotate text, will work for snapshots that are stored in the Zotero database, not for linked snapshots. The ability to markup a webpage, frozen in time as proof of what it once said, is quite a lure to paid storage. See Chapter 7 for more information on web snapshots in the Zotero Reader and Chapter 5 for instructions on the Zotero Connector.

Access to Attachments When Outside of Zotero

You may desire to access attachment files without going through Zotero. Perhaps a colleague wants to look at a document you have, and you want to send a link.

---

[8] https://www.zotero.org/groups

Linked attachments will exist in a file management system under your control. Whether on your hard drive, in the cloud, or both, you can find them and use them without having Zotero open on your desktop.

If you choose to store the attachments in Zotero, they will be on your computer, but they will be stored in a network of folders with coded names. The easiest way to retrieve the documents is to find the item in the Zotero ITEM LIST. Right-click and choose SHOW FILE. You can send the document to another as an email attachment.

LONG-TERM LOGISTICS

No matter which attachment option you choose, a full copy of your Zotero data will be on your computer.[9] And each attachment will be either on your computer or in cloud storage under your control. You do not need to worry that syncing to Zotero means you are losing control of your data. If something happened to Zotero and you could never sync again (highly unlikely, given its worldwide use), you would still have the working copy of the software on your desktop and a full copy of your data and all stored attachments.

You also have the export capabilities if you want to move to another product. It is important to know, however, that Zotero's export capacity does not include attachments. It will be easier to find attachments if you store them in your own cloud space and link out to them. But given Zotero's vital importance, it is highly likely some brilliant developers would arise to fill in this gap if anything happened to Zotero.

It's also important to know that Zotero has a utility that will take your linked attachments and store them if you decide to make a change down the road. It does not offer a utility to do the opposite.

---

[9] There is an exception to this. If you choose to store your attachments on Zotero's drive, but do not want a copy on your desktop unless something is immediately needed, you can set your syncing to "As Needed" in your SYNC SETTINGS and delete the PDFs from your own hard drive through your file manager's search function. I do not recommend this option.

10. QUICK GUIDE WRAP-UP

Congratulations! You have covered the foundational knowledge of Zotero—a tool that can support you in many types of research. It's a great tool for a student whose research ends at the end of this semester. It's a great tool for the seasoned researcher who will spend his or her career building on today's knowledge. And it serves everyone in between.

You know enough now to use Zotero effectively. If you learn nothing else, you are a much better-equipped knowledge manager for having made the effort.

Still, there is so much more you can learn, if you want to make Zotero all it can be in your field. I was some years into my Zotero use before it occurred to me that its tools could be harnessed to do clever things with the knowledge I was acquiring. I use Zotero's tools to create timelines, map legends, and research plans. It becomes my teleprompter (of sorts) while teaching online. When I imagine a way that viewing information differently might help me to find the patterns of knowledge I need, Zotero usually yields a way to do what I imagine.

If you have an interest in learning more, please stay tuned for more Quick Guides. They should follow soon after the publication of this guide.

I look forward to hearing about your growth with Zotero.

ABOUT ME

Donna Cox Baker

I retired from employment in 2021, after a first career in technical communications and a second in historical magazine and book publishing and teaching university-level history. A passion for genealogy first introduced me to history as a career and inspired me to get a PH.D. in the field, focusing on the history of the U.S. South and Southern religion. Soon after finishing my doctoral work, my interests turned back to family and local history. Realizing that I could not choose between history and genealogy as my niche, I finally created a place for myself (and my kind) at the spot where the two intersect. I call it GENOHISTORY and have a website at

GENOHISTORY.COM.[1] I created a small publishing company called Golden Channel Publishing from which to publish books, create tools, and teach genealogists and historians how to manage this hybrid knowledge. Zotero, which was my research lifeline in graduate school, came to be even more valuable to me in my genohistorical career. Introducing colleagues to Zotero has become a major part of my post-retirement third career.

A Quick Guide to Zotero 7 is my fifth book—four authored and one coedited. It is my third book on Zotero and is intended as the foundation guide to a series of Quick Guides now in the works. I encourage readers to SIGN UP FOR MY MAILING LIST[2] to be notified of the availability of these new books and to keep up with changes in Zotero.

Enjoy your Zotero journey!

Donna Cox Baker

---

[1] https://www.genohistory.com

[2] https://landing.mailerlite.com/webforms/landing/x2n4r0 or follow prompts at genohistory.com.

INDEX

www.ingramcontent.com/pod-product-compliance
Lightning Source LLC
Chambersburg PA
CBHW031221050326
40689CB00009B/1425